# A Teacher's Life

## Gordon Linnell

Summertrees

*A Teacher's Life*

© 1999 Gordon Linnell

First published in England in 1999
by
Summertrees
132 Summertrees Road
Great Sutton
Wirral
CH66 2RP

All Rights Reserved.
No part of this publication may be reproduced,
stored in a retrieval system, or transmitted
in any form or by any means, electronic,
mechanical, photocopying, recording or
otherwise, without the prior permission
of the Copyright holder.

A CIP entry for this book is avialable from the British Library

ISBN 1-872424-78-3

Printed and bound by
Bridge Books, Wrexham

# Schooldays

Down the echoing morning streets
Comes the future on pattering feet,
Schoolward rushing; flushing
From waiting doorways
Coveys of children.
Whirls and skirls of boys and girls
Dancing, prancing, glancing
Brighteyed at each other;
Sister, brother, rival, friend;
No end.
And, like a lively river,
Where the sidestreets meet,
Tributaries join the main stream
Of dreams, hurrying towards
Nine o'clock.

Jack Thomas

# Acknowledgements

My gratitude goes to the following, who willingly contributed to the book: Brian Aitchison; Jenny Aston; Les Aston; Arnold Banford; Jean Banford; Athol Barrington; Jo Barrington; David Brown; John Caswell; Roy Dale; Richard Dandy; Ann Daniels; Valerie Dixon; Ron Durdey; Ian Ellis; Ron Fleet; Ron Fletcher; Bob Fox; Alan Gaukroger; Fiona German-Lloyd; Anne Gittins; John Gough; Rose Graves; the late Philip Griffiths; Peter Harrison; Lesley Haskew; Paul Haskew; John Henderson; Beverley Henning; John Henning; Karen Henning; Linda Henning; James Hodkinson; Pat Howarth; Russell Jackson; Ken Jenkin; Huw John; Gareth Jones; Jean Jones; Jeff Jones; Jessie Land; David Leedham; Robin Leigh; Claire Lennie; Helen Lilley; John Marland; Simon Marland, at Bolton Wanderers F.C.; Sue Morton; Peter Murphy; Keith Muscott; Marilyn O' Neill, my good friend from the Sinatra Music Society, who suggested I write the book; Norman Peate; Malcolm Perry; Dennis Plackett; David Prince; Irene Proudlove; Janet Reddy; Romayne Roberts; Kathleen Rogers; John Sands; Di Sanna; Dick Sears; Brian Shepherd; Barrie Shore; Alan Swift; Debbie Tacon; Joanna Tacon; Penny Temple; Jack Thomas; Sarah Tinsley; Barbara Trevor; Chris Tune; Martin Turner; Steve Watson; John Weir; the late Elsie Whitson; Colin Williams; Gordon Williams; Julia Williams; Michael Williams; Alan Wolfenden; John Wolfenden; Douglas Wordsworth; Steve Yandell; the late John Young.

# Introduction

Certain images of West Street Infant and Junior Schools, nestling humbly in the grimy shadow of Crewe Railway Works, remain quite clear despite the passing of half a century. Nodder Sharratt's banana, for example. It seemed perfectly normal to Nodder to eat his banana in Mrs Holden's lesson, with his perennial two thin candles of snot running down into it. Mrs Holden, however, didn't quite see it that way; the confiscation of the offending fruit, plus a fair amount of the Sharratt mucus, ensued ... . The dragon of dragons Miss Alexander, whose resounding smack had one hapless little girl wetting herself on the spot ... Plump Miss Chadwick, wiggling her ample buttocks from side to side as she pedalled her ancient push-bike down West Street, children giggling and imitating the wiggle as she passed ... Singing sessions in the nearby Parochial Hall, the poignancy of *Early one morning*, the exuberance of *Dashing away with the smoothing iron* ... Nurse Broome, searching painstakingly for nits in the children's hair ... The unfairness of Miss Robinson, who knocked me two marks off a piece of writing because of a dot on the paper, a dot that was already printed into it! ... The school sports, especially the hundred yards race in which, the playground being only eighty yards long, the participants had to run full tilt into a brick wall then back for the last twenty yards! ... The trip to Stoke with Mr Kewley to see the City play West Ham — there weren't too many days out in those hard days not long after the war; and he bought us oranges! ... The class newspaper, when I gained control of the cricket page and filled the wall with photos of Denis Compton ... .

But it was in Mrs Burgess' class, when I was eleven, that the dream began, where first developed my fascination with the idea of writing on the board in all those coloured chalks, marking all those exercise books in red ink, correcting errors, awarding grades, writing comments; explaining things to the class, hopefully clearly and interestingly like Mrs Burgess did; there it was that a feeling of magic about the classroom, which never really left me over the next forty-odd years despite the occasional bout of cynicism along the way, first saw the light of day.

*To every pupil who tried*

# Chapter One

Crewe County Grammar School, a three-storey red-brick building in Ruskin Road, was opened in 1909. By 1952 it was a school of some 500 pupils, with most of the classes co-educational. For some reason, however, the first years were not, 1A being all girls, and my form, 1B, all boys. Mr Worgan was my form tutor and also took us for maths; a likeable, sympathetic man, and a good teacher.

Having been told before I went to the school, much to my alarm, that all first years had their heads forced down the toilets by older pupils, whereupon the chain was pulled (a kind of character-building initiation ceremony), I was relieved to get to the end of my first day without this happening. None the less, I returned home that September afternoon riddled with anxiety. On my timetable for day two was woodwork, which would involve my first encounter with a certain Mr P..... A group of second years had warned us that "Jasper," as he was nicknamed, was in fact one of the most horrible and frightening teachers the world had ever known. I duly met Jasper the following day. He was a short Welshman, with a parting down the middle of his black hair, of fearsome eyes, totally unsmiling.

"Come around 'ere!" he commanded fiercely in his South Walian accent, and we assembled apprehensively around the central bench in the room.

"Catch 'old of these!"

He proceeded to throw out, quite hard and very haphazardly, pieces of wood about a foot long, one of which every boy had to try to catch. If a piece thumped someone hard in the chest or clattered into the side of his head, this appeared to be of no concern to Jasper. When everyone was equipped with wood, he informed us that our first job was to plane the wood level, check it with a tri-square and then mark it 'face side' with the symbol that he demonstrated on a slab of wood he held out for us to note.

"Firstly you must determine the way the grain is going, then plane with the grain of the wood." He told us how to spot the direction of the grain, but I was far from convinced I would be able to do this with my own piece of wood. As ordered I clamped my wood in the vice and took hold of my plane. Now my maternal grandfather was a carpenter of great talent, a constructor, among other things, of sumptuous, ornate sideboards. Regrettably I inherited none of his gift. I began planing away laboriously. Moments later I felt a sharp pain on my right elbow. It was Jasper's cane, rapping away merrily. Then his voice screamed out

"You're planing against the grain!! You don't do it!!"

I was soon to discover that the latter was Jasper's catchphrase whenever he found someone doing something he didn't approve of. "You don't do it!" became part of the lingo of Crewe Grammar as we, outside of Jasper's hellish den, told each other off mocking the Merthyr Tydfil lilt:

"Riding on the wrong side of the road, is it? You don't do it!!"

"Handling the ball in the penalty area? You don't do it!!" And so on.

One poor lad, desperate to get his piece of wood level, planed and planed away, taking a bit off the front of it, then a bit off the back, more off the front, planing on and on until he heard screeched into his ear:

"You boy! Are you trying to make matchsticks?" That was about the nearest Jasper came to making a joke.

Sooner or later everyone in the form incurred Jasper's wrath for something or other, everyone felt the cane on the elbow or suffered the blood-curdling scream from a few inches away. And whatever he might have been in the bosom of his family, he seemed to us quite simply a heartless, humourless bastard. To the staff of the school, too, it seems. One of his ex-colleagues recently described him thus:

"A really nasty piece of work. Vicious and with more than a sadistic streak where pupils were concerned. He had no place in a civilised school like CCGS. He carried an almighty inferiority complex and compensated for it by his unpleasantness in the staff room — any new or younger teacher was fair game — and distressing methods in the classroom."

As is suggested in the quote above, Jasper and his like were, mercifully, in the minority at Crewe Grammar School.

Alec Walker (nicknamed 'Johnny' after the whisky; ironically he was a teetotaller) was a good man blessed with the knack of telling a story vividly and entertainingly. I was to get to know him well between the third year and the upper sixth as my teacher of Latin, but in year one Greek Mythology was his brief, and the fascinating if gory tales of such as Perseus and the Gorgon or Clytemnestra and Agamemnon held me enthralled. Johnny had his own highly idiosyncratic commando-style manner of entering the classroom. He would kick the door open, then, from the threshold, with his back to the class, observe their reflection in the glass windows of the upper part of the door. Then, when everyone was fully settled, he would enter, often with:

"Smells of boy in here — open the windows!"

The teacher who made the strongest impression of all on me that year was Raymond ('Dickie') Richardson, the music master. He had a great passion for his subject, which he taught in a rather unconventional manner. One lesson he marched into the room and with no preamble strode straight to the piano and played the opening chord of Hoagy Carmichael's *Stardust*.

"What a chord!" he enthused. "Gorgeous, isn't it?" Remarkably I can still hear that chord now, all these years later! His zeal was infectious — *Stardust* was the start of my life-long love affair with Carmichael's music.

Mostly, of course, the music was classical. New horizons opened up before me, seeds were sown for life. *The Polovtsian Dances* by Borodin, *The Planets* by Holst, Brahms' *Academic Festival Overture* (with Dickie's help I could go close to being able to follow a score of this), Bach's *Brandenburg Concertos*, the comparatively recent *Belshazzar's Feast* by Walton ... my world grew larger, my life richer.

Mrs Wright was my first French teacher. She was young, probably straight from college, and a pleasant person. Her first lesson with us, however, was certainly not the one I myself would have chosen to give to a first form some years later. There was no idea of hitting us with the French language from the start. We began with Mrs Wright telling us in English about France and asking if we'd been there. Then, as I recall, she drew a stylised mouth on the board and we had to imitate what seemed to me like farmyard animal noises as we pronounced what were apparently French vowel sounds.

By January we had a new French teacher, Mrs Hannah, wife of the long-serving geography master, he of the iron discipline; she, unfortunately, had little control over the class. Even I (normally well-behaved) had the temerity to reflect the sun light into her eyes by means of a protractor on one occasion. A stern verbal rebuke followed, but I escaped her regular punishment, which was to rap pupils' knuckles with the wooden back of a board-duster. There was not a great deal of work in the target language with Polly, as we called her. Once she asked a boy: "What's a white house?" hoping for the answer "une maison blanche, madame," but instead receiving the response "an igloo, miss."

However, in spite of Polly, I found French fairly easy and actually finished tenth out of thirty in the end of year exam, with a score of 82 per cent. None the less, I was to start the second year in the "C" stream. French was my only really good result; after passing the eleven plus I had erroneously come to the conclusion that I didn't have to try too hard any longer. Now I had to pay the penalty. My mother, so proud that I was at the grammar school, was enormously disappointed. "You've ruined my summer," she lamented. I determined to rectify the situation.

Miss O' Brien, in her early twenties, cut a rather glamorous figure in Crewe Grammar School. She had a pretty face with rather pouting red lips, a full bosom and a slim waist. French in 2C with her became something special; in addition to her physical attractiveness she was a fine teacher. French began to live for me, became the highlight of my week, something to enjoy and be successful at. In the early fifties French was taught mainly from a text book (Crewe used the now very quaint-looking series by Saxelby — *En Route, En Marche*, et cetera), but with Miss O'Brien we did plays as well, acting out rôles. It seemed almost like being in France ... and so, my desire to teach, born two years earlier, became more specific. I would teach French. I still have the exercise book from the time Miss O'Brien taught me; I note the impressive frequency with which she marked it.

I finished overall top of the third stream in the summer of 1954. My mother went into school to press for my promotion into 3B. This must have been extremely nerve-wracking for her; she was a very shy person. Miss O'Brien backed up the request, and I duly went up a class. In 3B I was able to continue my association with Miss O'Brien, but she was to disappear from my life for ever four months later.

In the Christmas exams I topped 3B, and was to be promoted to 3A, whose French teacher was Mrs Thompson. She was a beautiful woman, married to 'Jock' Thompson, who taught 3A maths. She was also rather prim and proper. On one occasion she remonstrated with two girls who had done a rather less than perfect job of brewing the tea for the teachers. Addressing the male members of the class, she announced:

"I hope that you boys note that these girls would make poor housewives."

Mrs Thompson was a competent teacher of French, and we did, as I remember, do a fair amount of conversation. But there was an unfortunate lack of drive about her, and somehow she did not have the 'magic' of Miss O'Brien.

In the meantime I had started Latin in September 1954, reacquainting myself with Mr Walker. As the only Latin teacher in the school, Alec Walker faced a daunting task. His class would often consist of three or four groups of people all at different stages of learning Latin, and he would have to deal with them all in the same lesson. Had I gone into 2B instead of 2C I would have started Latin in September 1953 (2A started German), but now, one year later, Alec Walker had to try to help me to catch up as quickly as possible. He became one of my favourite teachers at Ruskin Road, always, despite his hectic schedule (he had only one free period a week), seeming to have time for me. Under his guidance I learned Latin fairly rapidly, and by the end of the third year had progressed sufficiently for him to recommend my taking it in the fourth year. I had faith in his judgement and duly chose it in preference to a second science.

By the time I left the school the golden age of the widespread teaching of the classics in grammar schools was approaching its end; by the mid-sixties Alec Walker was left with a few crash courses in Latin for those needing it for university entrance. By then, most of his teaching was religious education; with no disrespect to this latter subject, this represented a sad end for a first-rate classical scholar.

The mid to late fifties was the real beginning of the television age. Alec Walker railed incessantly against television, saying he would never have a TV set in his house, only to be plunged into an agonising dilemma when the BBC announced they were to televise Sophocles' *Antigone* in the original Greek! In his desperate desire to see it, Alec had to compromise himself and get himself invited to the house of someone with a television!

Having finished second in French in 3A with 93 per cent I felt at the end of the year that things were going quite well for me linguistically. And, having achieved overall sixth place in the form, I had the satisfaction of knowing that my mother had renewed confidence in me. She was always a support to me in my studies and after that rather disastrous first year, had kept on encouraging me gently but firmly.

Crewe Grammar School had a remarkable assortment of teachers in the nineteen-fifties.

Miss Winifred Slee, Senior Mistress and biology teacher, resembled the actress Margaret Rutherford in appearance, except that she was much taller and more ungainly. She was charmingly naïve. Once, when she was carrying a box of fragile bones across the lab, it slipped from her grasp and crashed to the floor. Picking it up and examining its contents without even a "damn" or a "blast", she announced sadly: "Oh dear, they've all broken!" She seemed to have no idea, when she sat in front of her class in her skirt with her legs wide apart, that her pupils could see large expanses of her underwear.

Sometimes she seemed painfully insensitive to the feelings of her pupils. One girl went up to her and whispered something that the rest of the class could not hear. However, when Miss Slee quite loudly remarked: "What girl, what did you say? Ah, period problems!", everyone knew the poor girl's plight.

Part of her duties was to make sure the pupils in the assembly hall were quiet and ready for the Headmaster's entrance. Any fidgety girl would be admonished with "Jennifer — settle down, now!", even if her name were Sharon or Elizabeth! On one occasion a girl stumbled in late, carrying her bicycle pump into the hall (pupils were told not to leave them on their cycles since a number had been stolen), which was promptly confiscated by Miss Slee, on the grounds that such an object detracted from the solemnity of the occasion. Our Senior Mistress, however, proceeded to direct operations brandishing the offending pump, using it to point out any whispering or slouching pupils, much to the amusement of the staff gathered down the side and at the back! None the less, those same teachers thought the world of Miss Slee, who proved an excellent liaison officer between themselves and the Head. A whisper would come into their ear over 4pm tea in the staff room — what they had sought she had arranged.

Miss Slee shared a house with Miss Beech, a very competent maths teacher, who, despite her perpetually fluttering eyelids (much imitated by the children), was well respected. She may have looked meek and mild, but she had, in fact, plenty of backbone. Much smaller than Miss Slee, she could often be seen tapping some girl twice her size in the chest, indicating that such naughty ways (whatever they were) would not be tolerated; a contrite "Yes, Miss Beech" would follow.

'Jimmy' Jowett was the art master. He was not in my view particularly inspiring or imaginative and his discipline was rather lax. Sometimes we seemed to be drawing the same things for weeks on end — like Georgian buildings, for example. Jimmy was for the most part mild-mannered, but his occasional bouts of raging temper, including the berating of pupils, were *horribile visu*. Even more disconcerting, however, was Jimmy's trance. One moment he would be explaining to the class what he wanted them to draw or paint, the next he would be gazing vacantly out of the window, one hand still pointing to something on the board. This seemed to go on and on and on, with Jimmy staring into the distance. And then, as suddenly as it had begun, the trance was over. His focus returned to the business in hand; the lesson went on.

If the pupils of CCGS had run a survey on whom they considered to be the most odious bastard on the staff, the voting would have been close between Jasper and a certain Mr H. H was an English teacher I had the misfortune to have in years 2, 4 and 5. One had to have a certain amount of sympathy for him because of his asthma (he would sometimes have recourse to his inhaler during the lesson), but in truth he was a loathsome character. Like Jasper he was short in stature, like Jasper he was Welsh. When I was in 2C, he was looking for material to put in a magazine, and I had contributed a poem. My father had taken me to the Neil Franklin Benefit Match at Crewe Alex F. C. Many stars or ex-stars of the football world played in this game, including the Lion of Vienna himself, Nat Lofthouse. I wrote a poem about the game, and it took me quite a long time to do it. Now if H had said to me: "Well tried, but I don't think it's quite what I need for the magazine," I could have accepted this, despite being disappointed. But his scornful casting aside of the conscientious efforts of a sensitive thirteen year old was something I would never forgive him for. A superb example of how not to treat a pupil— at least I could learn from that for my own future.

He had a foul temper, too, regularly hitting pupils. One day Tubby Taylor crossed him. In an essay Tubby had, extremely riskily, written something uncomplimentary about H (Tubby was perfectly amenable and co-operative with other teachers), who now commanded him: "Take off your glasses, Taylor!" and proceeded to smack him viciously across his face.

H made me hate the literature I studied with him with a rare venom; this proved to be the only 'O' level I failed, despite the fact that we had the Headmaster (Harry Dowling) for Keats, which I loved. In my fifth year, however, H got his comeuppance. Everyone hated him to such a degree that we made the lessons sheer hell for him. In desperation he once hit Charlie Moorcroft across the face not with his palm, but with his clenched fist. And Charlie, seething from the injustice, came perilously close, in a moment of high classroom drama, to hitting him back. On another occasion, with the class uncooperative and noisy, H screamed: "If anyone else speaks, I'll hit Dixon!" My friend Wesley Dixon then tried to urge us on to misbehave, but we didn't; quite simply we didn't want to see Wes get thumped. H had saved his bacon by his dastardly tactic, but the detestation that 5A felt for him was now more acute than ever.

The war went on, and H was beginning to lose it. As the year progressed we developed a system. In those days the seat you were sitting on was attached to the desk in front of it by two metal bars which ran along the floor. During the first half of the English lesson we would edge forward gradually until, some half an hour later, we had almost pinned H to the board. Then, as the lesson wore on, we began to move backwards until, by its end, there was a vast space between H and the front desks. Such was our hatred of this man. It only went to show what could happen if a bright class should turn against a teacher; they can think of quite atrocious things to do.

Was there a saving grace about H? One girl said that as a sixth form tutor he was much better. The problem was, though, that he put a lot of people off English in the sixth form. My friend Alan Swift, for example, told me:

"I wanted to take English Literature in the sixth form, but when I went up to the room to ask about signing on and I saw H sitting there, I turned around and went and changed my options."

I often used to wonder what H must have been like as a colleague. Now I know.

"A most unpleasant little man, confrontational, quarrelsome, sneering and sarcastic. The only example I ever saw of fisticuffs in a staff room involved H. He attacked another teacher with flailing arms after some altercation or other. He relished picking on young or new members of staff, who were often too polite to retaliate with a senior colleague."

H died some years ago. No doubt he is now rotting in hell.

Tom Potts also taught English. He was a very well-spoken gentleman himself and hated slovenly speech in his pupils. If, for example, a boy were to come into the class to interrupt his lesson with the request: "Please sir, can I get me boowk out of me desk?" — then Tom would show considerable irritation. It was, of course, the pronunciation rather than the interruption.

"And what on earth is a boowk, boy? You mean book!" roared Tom, pronouncing it in the classic Oxford manner. "*My* book! *My* desk!" he shouted on, making the unfortunate individual say the whole sentence again, caring little for the embarrassment the boy might have been going through.

Personally I rather liked this larger than life character. Studying the cricket play *Badger's Green* and the espionage classic *The Thirty-Nine Steps* with him in the third year was a real pleasure, and my English grammar came on by leaps and bounds under his tutelage. On dinner duty he invariably said grace in Latin: "*Benedicat benedicator*," which pupils corrupted into "Benedicat benedicarthorse" or even "Bury the cat, bury the carthorse" when about to consume a Mars bar in the school yard. In my early years at Ellesmere Port I used Tom's grace when on dinner duty myself, to the bewilderment or amusement of some diners.

Tom was very keen on the *Eagle* comic which came out for the first time in the nineteen-fifties, especially the adventures of Dan Dare. He would come into the class on the day the comic came out and simply say "*Eagle*, boy" to someone he knew took it, whereupon, setting work for the class, he sat down to peruse the latest clash between his favourite astronaut and the dreaded Mekon.

And Tom had what must be one of the most impressive catchphrases any teacher ever invented: "Lock up the lips of loquacity with the key of contemplation."

Tom as a colleague? One source told me: "A witty man, a gentleman, and a superb gossip. Good fun at all night parties!"

The appreciation of Keats' poetry which Harry Dowling inculcated into me still endures, and I can still recall chunks of *Ode to a Nightingale*, *Ode on a Grecian Urn* and *St Agnes' Eve*, which he had us learn. As a Headmaster, though, he seemed rather remote. He would dash through the morning assembly at breakneck speed every day, breathlessly thanking God for the flowers and the birds, the woods and the fields, and so on, then walking briskly back to his study. It was the same, too, apparently, with his staff meetings; these were rare and soon over. Every afternoon at 4.01 he would be into his Rover and away. None the less the school that he ran was academically sound, most of the staff had few discipline problems, and there was for the most part a pleasant atmosphere.

The Head's policy at the time was to enter fourth formers for three 'O' levels a year early. I duly took maths, English language and French in

1956. I had had a few problems with maths when transferred to the top stream, but a combination of Jock Thompson's expertise and my mother's help saw me through to a good pass. French was no problem, but I passed rather unconvincingly in English; having H might, of course, have had something to do with that.

In year 5 I took 'O' levels in biology, history, geography, English literature and Latin, and began more advanced work in French (Guy de Maupassant short stories, for example) and maths (differential calculus—totally beyond me!). I was well taught in biology, history, geography and Latin, by people I liked and/or respected; I passed all four easily. I suppose now that I was stupid to let my dislike of H affect my efforts in English literature. I should have been less short-sighted, I should have thought of my future and got down to proper work in spite of my discord with the teacher. But at 15 or 16, somehow most young people can't see that far ahead and are adversely affected by their current prejudices. I suppose I was lucky to have seven teachers I could get on with and only one that I couldn't.

Overall I was not a trouble-maker at school and did not break too many rules. However, in June 1955, I was guilty of a transgression which, had the Headmaster found out, would almost certainly have resulted in my expulsion. It seems to me incredible now that I actually took the risk of running a book on the 1955 Derby. Half-pennies, pennies, twopences quickly came my way when the news got around that 'Honest Gord', as one friend wrote on my satchel, was taking bets on the race. Amazingly, since Peter O'Sullevan himself was tipping it, no one backed Phil Drake, who swept through the field to victory under French jockey Freddie Palmer. Mum and dad found out and rightly made known their displeasure, but none of the teachers knew, or if they did, they said nothing.

In my early years at Crewe Grammar I was a promising cricketer, my father, following his return from the Burma Campaign, having coached me for many hours, and with endless patience, in our back yard. Dad played for the team of the CWS clothing factory where he worked in Camm Street, and he was very hopeful I would make a good player. I have fond memories of the far-off days around 1950 when I would go with him to watch the games at Yew Tree Farm, Wistaston. I got to know other members of the team well, and they were always kind to me. Before play could start, the cows had to be shooed from the field, their excrement removed and the coconut matting laid for the wicket. Dad was a batsman, usually going in three or four, and was quite a powerful hitter of the ball. I recall one day when he made a sterling fifty and everyone began applauding him back to the pavilion; his modesty could scarcely cope and he just ran back all the way to get away from the attention.

Dad was keen that I should see some professional cricket, too. We went to Old Trafford to see Lancashire against New Zealand (1949) and India (1952), and to Aigburth to watch Lancs against the West Indies in 1950, when the peerless Frank Worrell stroked 150.

In my second and third year I was chosen as cricket captain of my form, and my father's hopes for me must still have been high. However, my fascination with horse-racing, which was to endure until I embraced the cause of animal rights in 1982, began at this time and rather took me over; I began to lose some of my zeal for cricket. This must have been an awful disappointment to him, since he had done so much to encourage me, but I did to some extent make it up to him later when I played regularly for Eastham on the Wirral.

In 1957, Mr Dowling, for the first time, apparently, insisted that sixth formers choose four 'A' level subjects rather than three. I had intended taking French, Latin and geography, but now added history. How lucky I did!

Geoff Hall, a tall man of military mien, came to Ruskin Road to teach geography after Billy Hannah's retirement. His daily routine was carried out with Teutonic precision. Upon his arrival he took lodgings in Franklin Avenue, a few minutes' walk from school. A friend of mine who lived opposite this house recounted how at 8.13 on the dot every morning Hall would walk down the drive, open the garden gate, check his watch, close the gate, then march onward to school.

Hall met a boy from school one Saturday morning in Crewe Public Library. The boy respectfully greeted him with "Morning, sir," but Hall was far from pleased with this. He told the boy to return to the end of the rows of shelves from which he had come, approach him again, and this time say "*Good* morning, sir".

During one lesson with the lower sixth I had the misfortune to see him administer a fearsome smack across Susan Williams' face. This was the only time I ever saw a teacher hit a girl at CCGS. She had, it seemed, been talking to a neighbour. These days, of course, Hall would have had serious consequences to face; in 1957, things were different. The incident terminated with *her* apologising to *him* for speaking out of turn in class!

I did not find Geoff Hall particularly likeable, unsurprisingly, but the main reason I asked to drop geography at the end of the Autumn Term of the lower sixth was that I was finding the 'A' level course much more scientific than I had anticipated and I found myself struggling. My request was granted.

History, on the other hand, seemed to follow on more logically from 'O' level and I felt I was faring reasonably well. The history teaching at 'A' level was shared by Mr Barker and Mr Utting. 'Bonzo' Barker was one of the elder statesmen of the school, a dignified part of its very backbone and solid foundation. He was a fine raconteur and always a fair and pleasant man. I can't recall his ever having shouted; he simply didn't need to. 'Faj' Utting (initials F. A. J.) was equally a gentleman. However, he placed rather too much reliance on the text book to be termed an inspiring teacher.

By now Miss O'Brien had left the school and the French 'A' level class was shared by Mrs Thompson and a new teacher, Mr Dennis Plackett. Dennis dressed in rather trendy fashion, had stylishly-cut blond hair, was good-looking, and it seemed that half the girls in the school were in love with him. He seemed to breeze into Crewe Grammar School, a veritable breath of fresh air among mostly ageing staff. I liked him, and soon recognised that underneath his very modern outlook and fashionable appearance lay a very solid teacher. I especially enjoyed the language work with him. I was, however, rather less gifted on the literature side and always feared this might affect my final result at 'A' level.

Continuing my association with Mr Walker for the 'A' level Latin course was a pleasure, and Virgil's Fourth Georgics came alive for me under his expert guidance. The poem is about bee-keeping, and studying it resulted in my having had the utmost affection and respect for the bee population ever since.

In the exams I needed two Bs and a C to get into Liverpool University to do Honours French. I didn't make it. I struggled throughout the French literature paper, never seeming to get momentum going, to get clear ideas down fluently. The language paper and the orals went rather better. I performed reasonably well in Latin and history, but certainly not brilliantly. I got three Cs. Liverpool was out, but I received two offers of a General Arts Degree course at Sheffield and Swansea. I accepted the Sheffield offer, and would continue with the same three subjects I had taken at 'A' level. Having recovered from the initial disappointment of not qualifying for Honours French, I was simply happy to be going to a university, and Sheffield, everyone told me, had a good reputation.

# Chapter Two

I have always felt that if a student can obtain the 'A' level grades necessary for entry into a university, then the degree, provided he or she maintains a decent work-rate, should be there for the taking. There is no doubt that 'A' levels are a stiffer test for an eighteen year old than the finals are for a 21 or 22 year old. I determined I would not waste my time at Sheffield, and indeed felt privileged to be there, to be able to continue my education under the guidance of academics several of whom, when they passed on some years later, were deemed of sufficient importance to have obituaries in the better newspapers.

It was Dr Collier who made the strongest impression on me; his lectures on the Theatre of the Absurd were quite riveting. I became something of an Ionesco fan, and a few years later, my zeal for the writer still fervent, I saw *La Cantatrice Chauve* and *La Leçon* at the celebrated Théâtre de la Huchette, the very cradle of Ionesco's art, in Paris. My grip on French literature began to tighten somewhat at Sheffield, but I still could not be classed as good at it, and I have to say that some of the prescribed books were not especially inspiring. Horace, Catullus, Ovid and Terence, however, the set Latin authors, proved stimulating and rewarding. History was very much my number three subject; I worked rather less hard at this, but was shrewd enough to make sure I held my own.

The academic work aside, I remember Sheffield most for its jazz. At the university itself there were festivals attracting well-known British groups, but it was the City Hall which became my mecca, as the big American names became regular visitors. I heard Duke Ellington, Count Basie, Oscar Peterson and George Shearing there, and most notably of all Ella Fitzgerald, then in her incomparable prime. Ella singing *Ev'ry Time We Say Goodbye*, poignantly, perfectly, to a rapt audience was unforgettable.

Having made sure that I was well-prepared for the final exams, I could almost enjoy them; I duly graduated in the summer of 1962 and enrolled for the Teaching Diploma course.

The education year involved three lots of teaching practice. My first, in September, was a two-week stint in a primary school in Attercliffe, one of Sheffield's less well-heeled districts. I was working under the aegis of a dedicated teacher called Mr Ellis; I fared moderately well, but could be faulted for the rather tentative nature of my efforts. In truth suddenly to find yourself the central point of a lesson, to have thirty-odd pairs of eyes trained on you after having, for the previous sixteen years, only had to contribute occasionally to the proceedings, was a rather daunting experience that it would take a lot more than two weeks to get used to.

My second practice was to have been at a secondary school in Sheffield, but circumstances changed this. My mother died in mid-October, just before the practice was due to begin. She had been diagnosed as having cancer of the lung in May and gradually faded away as the illness took control. She was a shy, modest woman, but always willing to serve others; she had certainly given me her time and her full encouragement with my studies, which made it all the sadder that she had been too ill to attend the degree ceremony during the summer.

Professor Armitage of the Education Department kindly arranged for me to do my practice at Nantwich Grammar School (whose headmaster he knew well), so that I could be with my father at this time, Crewe and Nantwich being just four miles apart.

Nantwich had had a grammar school since the seventeenth century, but the current building dated from 1860. The school was at the end of Welsh Row, near to the Shropshire Union Canal bridge, about half a mile from the town centre. The school's intake came not only from Nantwich itself, but from the leafy, attractive villages of South Cheshire, and for the most part they were very civilised young people.

I quite simply fell in love with teaching at Nantwich, feeling at home there almost from the start and sensing the keenness and pleasantness of the vast majority of the children I had dealings with. The staff, too, welcomed me warmly, although one or two things had to be gently explained to me. On my first day I had put my overcoat on a certain peg in the staff cloakroom only to be told that that particular peg had been used by a certain teacher (and only by him) for a considerable number of years. And, having collected in my first set of exercise books, having taken them into the staff room and installed myself at a certain seat to begin marking them, I was approached by a very nice gentleman who explained to me in a very cultured manner that Mr Gowanlock, a much revered senior teacher, had been using that particular marking space since 1920!

I was given lots of valuable advice by the Nantwich staff. French master Jack Clifford noticed that I had set too hard a homework to a second year set, resulting in most of them finishing with 3 or 4 out of ten.

"You've got to give them success. If the homework's hard, help them more before they go home to do it. You've got to judge it so that most of them get a good mark." A sound tip; now I know all too well that success builds confidence and confidence leads to more success.

John Jones was amicable and just as helpful with advice on teaching Latin grammar. He had replaced the infamous 'Dico' (I never found out his real name) as Head of Latin in the school. Dico had acquired his sobriquet because 'dico' was the Latin verb he most regularly beat (quite literally) into his pupils. As he belaboured some poor lad's backside, he would recite the principal parts of the verb to him in unison with the blows:

"Dico, dicere, dixi, dictum, learn it, lad, learn it, lad!"

Things, mercifully, had moved on from that. John Jones was an *âme sensible* who did not, as far as I saw or knew, hit pupils.

Head of History Ted Lloyd was another to give good counsel, encouraging me away from the text book and into the practice of telling the story oneself, which makes the topic or event much more vivid to the pupils.

The Headmaster, Mr Frank Morris, was very kind and supportive. He lived in a house adjacent to the school, and the first year pupils (known on the Nantwich system as year III), were partly taught in rooms of his house! I taught III Kent there for French; it was quite a unique atmosphere. Frank Morris was a very keen cricketer, and quite proud of his school's teams. I was told that this pride could be carried a little too far at times; he could be rather unprofessional in assembly, for example, if things had gone wrong in matches against other schools. Remarks such as "Due to the incompetence of the Northwich umpire, the first eleven lost by two wickets at Sir John Deane's on Saturday" were not uncommon.

Mr Morris introduced the idea of having classical music played in the hall every morning before assembly; it proved a very civilised way to begin each day.

Just as my allotted four weeks at the school were coming to an end, it was announced that Miss Ling, a French teacher who had been taken ill, would not be returning before Christmas. I volunteered to stay a further two weeks until the end of term. I didn't have to return to Sheffield until January and I was enjoying Nantwich enormously; Mr Morris was pleased to accept my offer. During that fortnight, I felt I really became a part of the school. I went to several of the year group parties, to a staff party and to the carol concert in St Mary's Church, when the whole school trooped down Welsh Row and into town, as they had done every year since the school began.

My Nantwich idyll duly came to its end just before Christmas. Six weeks of learning a lot, of fulfilment, of fun, of growing to like a large number of young people I would never forget. Saying goodbye to the Remove (Third Year), whom I had taught for both French and Latin, was notably poignant. Any other thoughts about my career that might have crept into my mind, like being a sports commentator or a journalist, were decisively cast aside. Teaching would be my life.

Under the good guidance of the Head of French Mr Otley, I came through satisfactorily in my third practice at Rowlinson Technical School in Sheffield, where I had my first taste of teaching all-boy classes, finding the Yorkshire lads likeable and quite easy to get on with. But some of the teachers I observed at Rowlinson struck me as being very uninspired, and I noted the classes' indifferent reaction to this. I could learn from what I saw; if the teacher doesn't make the effort, what chance is there that the pupils will?

In the spring of 1963 I lost out at three interviews for French posts: at Crewe Grammar School (to my best friend Wesley Dixon), at Lymm Grammar School (interviewing quite well but going under to an experienced teacher) and at Darwen Grammar (interviewing badly).

It was pouring with rain when I arrived in Ellesmere Port on a day in early June. My interview was at the local boys' grammar school, which was a comparatively new establishment. The school was in the Whitby district of the town, situated on the Chester Road some two miles away from the town centre. I met the Headmaster, Mr Kenneth Hedges, and the Head of French, Mr John Sands. I discovered that the other two applicants had withdrawn from the interview; it seemed I was the only one left! I interviewed reasonably, Mr Hedges telling me that his friend Mr Morris, whom he had phoned, had spoken well of me. However, he said, he did have some qualms about appointing me.

"You look so young!" he declared candidly. By now, that is, June, people already teaching could not leave their posts to take up another appointment for September; the final date for giving notice was May 31st. Therefore either a novice or someone coming back into teaching would have to be appointed. If Mr Hedges was hesitating, this fact ought to work in my favour, but it looked as if he might still postpone making an appointment.

John Sands asked me to come up to his classroom and watch his lesson, stationing me at the back of the room.

"It's a first form," he said, "they're not bad." I was to find out later that when John Sands said something was "not bad," it usually meant that it was very good. And so it proved. 1W were to my eyes and ears very smart performers. It was John Sands' own exhibition, however, that was a revelation to me. What energy! What panache! What inspiration! And all in the target language! 1W were clearly learning fast and enjoying every minute of it. I sat spellbound for twenty minutes, knowing already that this driving style had had a profound influence on me and would most certainly be incorporated into my own method of teaching the foreign language.

"Now you try!" suggested John, putting me right on the spot. I did my best to maintain the momentum, and the pupils did react positively. Twenty further minutes later, the bell went, the class were dismissed, John and I returned to the Head's study. I was informed that I had the post from September.

Afterwards, David Brown, a teacher of German, came and introduced himself to me in the staff room. Very well spoken, tall, tweed-jacketed, pipe-smoking, very open and friendly, Dave drove a white MG sports car at the time and offered me a lift back to Chester. The ride proved an exhilarating one. Dave drove very fast, thoroughly enjoying the performance of his conveyance.

"Bloody marvellous car!" he enthused. Over the next few years I would hear the phrase "Bloody marvellous!" often from Dave's lips. Dave was residing at the YMCA in Chester at the time and wondered if I would want to stay there too from September. He said he could give me a lift to school and we could share the petrol costs. I saw the General Secretary; it was all arranged. The YMCA was a large Georgian building overlooking the River Dee in Chester, with accommodation for about 40 residents.

Many Ellesmere Port Grammar staff stayed there in the early stages of their career.

By September Dave had changed his MG for a red TR3, which he drove with all the flair and aggression with which he had driven the MG. Journeys were invariably eventful; he would often hit 90 mph on the way to school and he showed notable impatience with anyone blocking his path — "Get out of the bloody way!!"

Dave had endless enthusiasm for Chester; we'd often walk around town after school.

"Bloody marvellous, Chester! Never get tired of walking round it!" One evening we walked into the cathedral to find the Hallé Orchestra rehearsing for an imminent concert there.

"Vaughan Williams, Gordon. Listen to this!" Within minutes Dave's fervour for the music had spread right over me as the notes of the *Fantasia on a Theme by Thomas Tallis* drifted gloriously heavenwards. I soon acquired Sir Malcolm Sargent's version of the piece and got to know it well. Later I was to become familiar with much more of VW's music, including the symphonies, but that autumn afternoon in Chester Cathedral, with Barbirolli in command, was where the enchantment started.

# Chapter Three

Ellesmere Port Grammar School was opened in September, 1959, an occasion for great civic pride. The more academically talented children of its borough would no longer have to make the journey to the Wirral Grammar Schools in Bebington. The new school contained at the outset three years of boys and girls.

In reality it was scarcely ready for its opening. Several staircases still had no handrails, the Trinidad Asphalt Company were still laying the tarmac in the playground, and there was no proper staff room or Headmaster's office. The Head and the staff shared a classroom divided by a flimsy partition. Neither was there a canteen; everyone had to bring sandwiches. The hall was not completed; there could be no assemblies for several weeks. The games fields were not ready; other fields in the area had to be hired. It was to be several weeks before the building itself was in proper order, and the best part of two years before the playing fields were completed.

The school's catchment area included not only the borough of Ellesmere Port but also districts on the outskirts of Chester— Upton, Boughton, Huntington, Christleton, Vicar's Cross and Saughall.

A term before my career began, the adjacent Girls' Grammar School opened, taking away the majority of the school's female intake, leaving just the sixth form girls to complete their studies in what was now the Boys' Grammar. The playgrounds became segregated; boys and girls below the sixth form ostensibly came together only on the school buses, which the two schools shared. And it was only on bus duty that the staff of the two schools came into professional contact.

What had happened was not popular. Pupils, with the staff's approval, had some months previously sent a petition to County Hall strongly objecting to the segregation of the sexes. In the editorial of the 1963 school magazine published before the end of the 1962-3 academic year, Beverley Hearnden and Lynleigh Owens had stated their case powerfully and lucidly:

> In a co-educational school the learning of basic facts is supplemented by an understanding of people, and surely the latter is the foundation of an education which is to fit a person for the life he or she is going to lead. Since most primary schools and all universities are mixed, we fail to understand why, during the impressionable years of our lives, we are forced to live in a community which does not exist outside school.

The county, of course, did not listen. Eleven years later, however, when the school turned comprehensive, it became mixed. Beverley and Lynleigh would no doubt have smiled ruefully at that.

There is all the difference in the world between being a student on a teaching practice and being a probationary teacher. As a student I often had the class teacher in the room observing (these days this is obligatory), so the pupils were unlikely to misbehave with an established teacher there. A probationer, however, would be visited by the Head of Department twice during his or her first year, that would be all. The rest of the time the novice teacher was alone— you had to sink or swim. There were to be many occasions during my first year when I was sure I was sinking.

For my first year my timetable would be restricted to the first three year groups. I would teach 3P (the fourth stream) for five 40-minute lessons a week, 3D for four lessons (they were the second stream). Both classes contained boys with reputations for trouble. In the second year I had 2S (second stream) and 2I (third stream). I was to teach 1C and 1T (unstreamed) in the first year. I had four free lessons to be used for marking and preparation, although these became liable to be reliefs if anyone was absent, and two periods of games with year two.

All my classes were to use the Whitmarsh French Course text books. It seems to me incredible now, with all the cassettes, videos, worksheets, flashcards, OHTs, realien, *Fun with French* items on the computer as well as the large, full-coloured course book, that in 1963 even the reel-to-reel tape recorder was in its early days and in essence the teacher's only resources were the rather drab-looking Whitmarsh and a piece of chalk!

My first lesson was with 2S. I had been told that the first thing to do was to compile a list of their names for my markbook. These days you receive a computerised sheet with this information on it, so you can go straight into the foreign language at the start of the lesson. In 1963, however, things were different. I was a novice and I did what I was advised to do.

"Who's first on the register?" I asked. A boy raised his hand.

"And your name is ... ?"

"Bastard!" I thought I heard him say. This rather set me back. Were they fooling around already?

"Pardon?"

"Bastard, sir!"

A bright-looking boy near the front rescued me.

"It is, sir. That is his name." I thanked him.

"How do you spell it?" I asked the first boy.

"B-A-R-S-T-A-D." Not quite what I thought, but near enough!

My markbook for 1963-4 (I've kept all 35 of them) tells me there were 33 boys in 2S, which large number didn't make it any easier in class or in the marking of their books. But in truth most of them were good lads and a lot of them were not bad at all at French.

Kevin Hughes, though, was a problem. I don't doubt that had I taught him later in my career I could have dealt with him more effectively, but as a newcomer I found him difficult. One particular lesson he was sitting on the back row and started to mess around. I was trying to teach the whole class at the time and was put out of my stride by this disruption at the other end of the room. Suddenly I felt something snap inside me and I marched down the aisle to where Hughes was sitting, whereupon I smacked him one across the back of his head. Unfortunately, however, at the moment of impact my watch fell from my wrist and smashed into what seemed like a thousand pieces on the floor under Hughes' desk. The humiliation of it! I recall saying something like:

"Don't just sit there, Hughes, help me pick up my watch! And you others, turn round! I don't think it's funny!" How not to teach, lesson one. Hitting a pupil has been illegal since 1986; in the sixties, however, it was still used to a degree. Some staff used a slipper, others clipped boys round the ear, there was knuckle-grinding on pupils' heads, ear-twisting and chalk or board-duster throwing! I myself smacked a few when I had been driven too far and didn't have the expertise to deal with the situation in a better way. Looking back now I wince at some of the things I did and hope that the boys concerned have forgiven me. One colleague, who often dealt in scathing sarcasm, advised me that a teacher could be far crueller with words than by hitting a pupil. In truth I had no wish to be cruel; I thought a quick smack, over in a second, was better than a wounding tirade which could affect a pupil for years. I could never have caned a boy in cold blood; it chills me now to recall Deputy Head Dennis Holman addressing the morning assembly with the words:

"Any boy caught trespassing on the rugby pitches will be beaten."

I reckon that in all I smacked about fourteen boys out of the thousands I had to deal with in lessons or on duty or generally around the school. As a percentage it is very small, but it is still fourteen too many, and I find myself in admiration of those who never hit a pupil. John Henderson, my colleague for 33 years, was such a teacher.

"I made myself a golden rule when I started that I would never hit anyone, and I stuck to it," he told me simply.

Ellesmere Port Grammar School was, in fact, a happy school, as visitors often remarked. Most pupils never needed physical reminders to get them to toe the line; they were readily cooperative. And in the case of most of those who did get hit occasionally, their attitude was rather different from that of some of the young people of today. Then, I'm sure, most boys did not even tell their parents that they had been hit by a teacher; indeed, if they did, they ran the considerable risk of having the punishment repeated by their father or mother. Pupils were not so obsessed by their rights in the sixties; they took it for the most part without whingeing if

their ear was clipped and few grudges were borne. *O tempora, o mores!* Recently a colleague, seeing a boy being silly and blocking a corridor, gave him a fairly gentle push from behind only to find the eleven year old whipping round in front of him, pointing his finger aggressively and snarling:
"If you touch me, I'll f...ing have you!"

Obviously no one wants a school where children are badly abused, but surely the pendulum has swung much too far the other way in this age of 'child power'.

Mr Hedges himself, as his long-serving secretary Elsie Whitson recently confirmed to me, made sparing use of the cane and really hated having recourse to it. A man of quiet strength, he rarely shouted but he had an aura of considerable authority none the less. He had served in the Indian Army (reaching the rank of major), and had run the army cadet corps in his previous school, Bedford Modern. His talents extended into the musical and sporting fields; he had played French horn in the Bedford Symphony Orchestra and had been awarded a blue for swimming at Cambridge University.

His aims for EPGS were made clear from the start; he wanted the pupils to have a broad education in a forward-looking school with a strong technical department; further, he wanted to offer a wide range of sporting activities. He introduced rowing, which brought him both praise and criticism. The disapprovers thought that he was trying to make the school too much like a public school whilst at the same time watering down the sporting talent which could have been directed towards rugby, soccer, cricket or athletics. In fact the rowing club proved a great success, bringing much kudos to the school.

Mr Hedges was also accused of imitating the public schools in the dining hall. The fact that he termed the head cook 'matron' does not in fact prove anything, since all Cheshire Grammar Schools were instructed to use this title at the time, but the use of the server system for school lunches was very much a public school feature. Each table had eight diners, two of whom would act as servers, bringing the food over from the serving hatch in large rectangular metal containers, and then serving a plateful to each person at the table. Grace was always said before anyone could begin his repast. As a social exercise the procedure had some value, and Mr Hedges invariably overruled suggestions from some staff that the cafeteria system would be more practical. The server system was somewhat cumbersome and time-consuming, however, and the final sitting sometimes did not end until after the start of the first afternoon lesson.

History master David Leedham caused some amusement at a staff meeting when suggesting that a mobile podium be introduced, which would enable staff to move swiftly around the dining hall to check pupils' behaviour and also allow staff who, like David, were shortish in stature, to be clearly seen by all pupils in the hall. Alas, the suggestion was never taken all that seriously, and the potentially awesome sight of a teacher zooming around between tables calling sloppy eaters to order failed to materialise.

In the seventies, however, the old system was finally abandoned and the more efficient cafeteria method, much to the relief, it must be said, of most of the staff, was introduced.

Mr Hedges sometimes used terminology redolent of the public school. One morning, for example, seeing a boy copying homework from another, admonished him sternly with: "You boy, you're cribbing your prep!" And in assembly it should be noted that we used the *Public School Hymn Book*.

So perhaps Mr Hedges did see certain features in the public school ethos that he wanted to bring to his suburban grammar school; none the less, those who knew him best affirmed that he was far happier in the more egalitarian ambiance of EPGS than he had been in the private school atmosphere of Bedford Modern.

Head teachers at the time still saw themselves as being part of the teaching staff, and Mr Hedges taught geography (his main subject), maths and musical appreciation. This proximity to the 'chalk face' enabled him to be fully aware of the attitudes and needs of the pupils he had in his school, an advantage which later Heads, who had to be so submerged in administration that having any kind of a teaching timetable was an impossibility, could never enjoy.

The two third year classes I had were both proving difficult. With 3D I made mistake after mistake, sometimes trying to be strict, at others trying, inopportunely, to bring humour into the lessons. I started to shout at them, increasingly loudly and more frequently, which made them worse.

"You are like a bad actor!" Gérard the French assistant told me, which hurt somewhat at the time, but which later I could see all too clearly was true. 3P were not much better. My control over them felt very lax most of the time. With both classes I felt that I was failing.

Then another outburst against a pupil took place. Instead of ignoring a blatant display of dumb insolence by a boy in 2I, I determined to settle his hash — without hitting him. I marched over to his seat and, cretinously, grabbed him by his hair, yanking him upwards. Catastrophically, a huge tuft of his hair came away in my hand! I slipped it into my pocket and then surreptitiously into the YMCA dustbin when I got home. And that night I really did think my teaching career was over. Someone told me that the boy's father was one of the top men at County Hall, which turned out to be true. I expected the worst: the next morning I would be called into the Head's office, the boy's father would be there, I would have to endure a full investigation into the incident, there would be a court case ... In fact, nothing happened. Either the boy did not tell his father, or, if he did, the latter played hell with him for getting into trouble. But surely he must have noticed his son's bald patch?!! The mystery remains unsolved.

I had a fair measure of success with the first years I taught in 1963-4, 1T and 1C. Right up to the end of my career, I got special enjoyment from teaching that year group, catching them, as it were, at their keenest and most impressionable. Seeing them bouncing out of their seats with enthusiasm and willingness to participate never failed to stimulate my own fervour.

Our assistant Gérard Guéguen was from Lorient in Brittany. Like myself he took a room at the YMCA, and being of similar age and having plenty in common, we became good friends. He introduced me to the music of Georges Brassens and Jacques Brel; some of their lyrics I can still recite now. For my part, later in the school year I introduced Gérard to cricket. This was not easy to start with; he was under the impression that the two batsmen were on opposite sides! Eventually, however, we made progress and Gérard had the honour of playing for the staff cricket team. Gérard had a sense of humour that I liked. Whenever he had to give his name in shops he was invariably asked to spell it, since Guéguen would be unfamiliar to most English people. He became rather tired of this, and determined to do something about it. He knew he didn't look English, so he had to choose a foreign name he thought would be easy to spell. And so, in a dry cleaner's in Brook Street, he gave in a jacket to be cleaned.

"Name, please?"

"Baldini," said Gérard as I exploded with laughter behind him.

"How do you spell it?" asked the woman.

Since there were a large number of young foreign people living in Chester, including at the YMCA and YWCA, the YMCA management decided in the autumn of 1963 to found the International Club. This was, in effect, a Saturday night dance to which all residents could go. Gérard and I became regulars. One night in October, much to our surprise, a group of sixth-form girls from EPGS walked into the club. One of these, Ann Thompson, made a bee-line for Gérard, who seemed happy enough with this situation. All professional considerations seeming suddenly to be cast aside, I felt myself drawn like a magnet towards the very pretty Brita Johnstone, who, for her part, was giving me plenty of encouragement. They came again the next Saturday and we began to date them. I didn't actually teach Brita, of course, and the age difference between us was quite small. None the less I knew that what I was doing was looked askance upon in certain quarters. John Sands found out, and, taking me to one side in the staff room one day, stated quite clearly:

"I'd no more think of doing what you're doing than jumping in the lake!"

The intimacy between Brita and myself did not go beyond moderate petting; at that period I was a committed Christian and the idea of sex before marriage was against all my principles. In fact I wore a 'Jesus saves' badge on my jacket lapel. One lesson, when I was becoming angry with a boy in 2S and threatening to deal with him in no uncertain manner, he pointed mischievously to the badge, reminding me 'Jesus saves', and disarming me totally, to the amusement of the rest of the class.

Gérard, meanwhile, had moved from Ann Thompson to Jenny Killcross, another International Club attender, with whom he became quite smitten. Jenny, however, was not taking the romance quite as seriously, and after a couple of months or so, wanted the relationship to end. When she told Gérard this, he became distraught, going round to her house one night and threatening to commit suicide. Jenny did not take the threat seriously, though, and her judgement was proved correct. One week after his visit, Gérard was dating a third sixth-former, Anne Tunner!

I got to know Brita's parents well, and Brita began coming to the Grosvenor Park Baptist Church with me quite regularly, where she was warmly accepted by my friends. Gradually, however, the relationship began to wilt, and may not have had much further to run when it was ended at the most remarkable staff meeting in the history of the school.

Mr Hedges, sombre-faced, addressed his staff as follows:

"It has come to my knowledge that seven members of staff are taking out sixth form girls. This practice must stop immediately. I want to see all

*Brita*

the seven members of staff concerned in my study before the end of the day."

Seven! I had known that Gérard and I were not the only transgressors in this matter, but I hadn't realised there were as many as seven of us! Defiantly I held out until the next day, when I went to see the Head.

"Look, Mr Linnell," he began (he normally called me by my christian name), "you don't really think this relationship is going anywhere, do you? Don't you realise these girls are very immature?"

And so my attractive companion and I said goodbye. Ironically, however, not all seven of the relationships ended; three of my colleagues went on to marry the girls concerned.

As my first year entered its final two months, I was still having plenty of problems with the third years, 3D in particular. I was not the only one having trouble with this class, however; they had got themselves quite a reputation by now. It was determined that they would have all the well-known strict disciplinarians on the staff as their teachers in year 4. That meant John Sands as far as French was concerned; it also meant that I had to contain them for only a few further weeks.

I realised that once a teacher has 'lost' a class, it is almost impossible to get them back. I had quite a humiliating experience with them in a relief lesson two years later, by which time I was well-established with the forms of year four and below. This form, now 5E, remembered me from my novice days and gave me a poor reception when I walked in to cover the lesson. Many, many years later, however, I was to meet two of them at parents' evenings, when I taught their children. It pleases me to be able to say that they both achieved good results and their fathers (my former 'enemies') were very grateful for my helping them effectively.

Between September 1963 and the spring of 1964 I had found out a lot. Shouting at classes, for example, should never become a habitual event, rather a shock tactic to be used sparingly. Looking uncertain in front of a class is another taboo. It is easy to say this after years of experience; as a newcomer to the job it can be very difficult to teach brimming with confidence. I had (and have) a shy streak in me; in my later days I could act my way through that, whereas in the early stages I often felt myself going red and feeling unsure. The nicer kids were sympathetic, but there were a fair number of not so nice ones who took advantage of what they perceived as a weakness and caused problems.

John Sands came in to watch me twice during the year, not being all that impressed with my lesson with 3D early on, but expressing some satisfaction when he watched me take 2S some time later. John was a tough taskmaster, always taking pains not to overpraise, but he was not only the inspiration that I had observed on the day of my interview, but also an ever-willing help whenever I needed advice about the teaching itself or about French grammar, on which his knowledge was superb.

John Wolfenden was a further help to me. He had begun his teaching career a year before me, and was clearly quicker to learn the ropes than I had been. I learned from John the importance of keeping calm as a teacher; John never seemed to get flustered or let pupils wind him up. Whatever happened he seemed to remain serene and fully in control. He was a fully-involved member of the school community, being not only a well-respected teacher of French and German but also taking over the rowing club when Mike Harrison left, and contributing enormously to its success. Even John had one very uneasy moment with a class, however; he told me of his own blushing when he committed a highly infelicitous Spoonerism on *"Ich habe keinen Hund,"* which had a third year class tittering stupidly. A teacher who is now very well established in the school is David Bell. He once related his own unsureness and embarrassment when first facing a class of sixth form girls for geography; he was so shy that he conducted the whole lesson talking to the blackboard rather than turning and making eye contact with the girls.

And so, somehow, I managed to get through my probationary year. It had been partly an enjoyable experience, but undoubtedly a considerable ordeal.

However, the humiliation I had suffered made me determined that I would do better in my second year. Any new classes would be dealt with sympathetically but very firmly. I would have more confidence now that I had been through the whole thing once. I would learn from my errors. Any class that I would have to continue with that I had made mistakes with I would make the best of, hoping they would toe the line properly eventually.

One pleasing thing happened before the end of the year. One of the more civilised boys in 3P, who was being promoted to 4W in September, asked me:

"What fourth year will you be taking next year?"

"4W," I replied, dreading what he might say next.

"Good. I was hoping I would have you again."

I couldn't believe it. I knew I had made something of a mess of teaching 3P, but this boy had faith in me. Thanks for that, Malcolm Jeffries— I will never forget the boost you gave me.

## Chapter Four

4W was made up of 34 boys, some of whom, like Malcolm Jeffries, had been in 3P the previous year, and a few of these, unlike Malcolm, had caused me problems in their third year. There were in addition one or two I didn't know who had a reputation for trouble; things therefore would not be entirely straightforward. I retained 2S (now 3S) and 2I (3I) in their entirety. In the second year I was to take 2D, made up of several of the previous year's 1T and 1C, plus some I had not met. In Year 1 I had 1L and 1Y.

1L was my own form. The lettering of forms at EPGS was simple; they were named after the first letter of their form-teacher's surname. First years were mixed ability groups to be streamed according to their year's work and the results of their exams the following summer. I desperately wanted 1L to have a good reputation; I wanted their behaviour to be as perfect as it could be. I therefore paid every attention to detail— appearance, uniform, the way they sat (not slouching), the way they came in, the way they went out, the way they went around the school, their standard of writing and the quality of their work. I was prepared to try every inch of the way to make them into a good form, and it really did pay dividends. Inculcating good habits into 11–12 year olds will reap rewards not only in their first year, but, hopefully, for the rest of their school career, too. To me 1L were special from the outset, and I wanted them to feel that. I wanted them to know that I cared about them, that it was important to me that they did well at all their work, not just French, that they developed their sporting or musical talent or whatever gifts they had in other areas. I wanted to be proud of them and told them this. At the end of the year, of course, I lost some of them to the streaming system, but when I inherited others to take their places in the autumn of 1965, I tried to set the standards and rules all over again. These lads would be my form for the next four years, and I remember them now as the most special class of my whole career.

They were not, of course, perfect. I got to hear of horseplay they got up to in some lessons, how they took apart a new music teacher, for example, and I let them know in no uncertain manner what I thought of this. But in truth they did little wrong in my presence.

I passed my driving test in 1966 and started taking groups of the form in the car on various excursions. North Wales mountains became a fairly regular Sunday jaunt; we went to Manchester United (these were the days when you could just walk in without booking— we saw a 20-yard Bobby Charlton thunderbolt almost break the net during United's 2-0 defeat of Sheffield Wednesday), to Everton (I'll never forget the look of wonder on Robert Pollard's face when we reached the top of the stand stairs and he looked out over the whole ground); to Stoke City (in the top division then); to Beeston and Peckforton Castles; to the *Playhouse* in Liverpool (I crashed the car into the back of a van on the way and was stupid enough to drive through the Mersey Tunnel twice with a leaking radiator but lucky enough to get away with it!); and to Crewe Railway Works (with a sense of pride that my home town held some interest for my young friends).

I also found out about a supposedly haunted house on the Denbigh moors near Pentrefoelas, and, with special parental permission, took four of them one winter night to visit it. It was a ruined mansion of some size, set back a few hundred yards from the main road, accessible by a winding path. We explored it tentatively to begin with, using torches, then found a way up onto the roof. Obviously I wasn't going to let them endanger themselves climbing all over it in the dark, and we returned to ground level. A few minutes later we received something of a shock; a torch shining its way up to the mansion from the path we had followed. And with the torch, shortly afterwards, two men in uniform could be discerned.

"You're all under arrest!" a Welsh voice announced. "We have reason to believe that you have been up on the roof stealing lead!"

He addressed me. "Your name?"

"Gordon Linnell."

"Well then, Gordon," he continued, "have you anything you wish to say?"

"Well, actually, we were looking for a ghost."

"Oh, really? Do go on."

"We'd heard that the old mansion was haunted by the ghost of the Duke of Devonport."

They smiled at each other. "And what were you doing on the roof?"

"Well, we were just exploring," I replied, hesitantly, feeling more and more like Just William every minute. "Actually, we're from Ellesmere Port Grammar School, and these boys are my pupils."

"Indeed?"

Some time later, having explained to us that recently there really had been lead-thieves visiting the mansion, they let us go, making it clear that a return to the house would not be advisable.

When 1Y became 2Y in September 1965, they were the top stream and I was lucky enough to be entrusted with their education in French. This proved to me that John Sands had fully accepted me now; letting me take a top stream bristling with academic talent was a real honour. It seemed that in those days Heads of Department kept most of the top streams for themselves. Teaching this class was a terrific experience; their quick, lively minds and ready response, their excellent and imaginative written work, their humour ... they were never academically bettered by any I taught subsequently.

Most boys at EPGS spoke the Queen's English reasonably well, some with a slight Liverpool twang, others with a more pronounced Scouse accent. But there were very few who talked what would be termed 'posh'. There was one boy, however, who was in 1Y but failed to make it into the top stream the following year, who had a decidedly far-back accent. Once we were doing a French play in which two burglars were interrupted whilst robbing a flat by the owner who shot one of them in the shoulder. To heighten the drama I had brought in a gun with caps. When the gun went off, our far-back friend leapt out of his seat, clapped his hands and exclaimed:

"Oh I say, sir, this is super!"

That same boy had a rather obsequious side to his character. Once, when handing in his geography book to my colleague Dave Ingram, he pronounced:

"My essay, sir, I think you'll find it rather good!"

Dave told me he gave him four out of ten.

Another boy, named Buchanan, also had a somewhat plummy voice. Once, on a rainy day when the ball had become very greasy, he was taking a throw-in in a football game I was refereeing. As he raised his arms to take the throw, the ball slipped backwards out of his grasp.

"Oh, fack!" he exclaimed. The other lads fell about laughing. I pretended not to hear, but they must have seen the smirk on my face.

"Just take it again, Buchanan," I said.

At this time the GCE examination had grades 1–9, with 1–6 being passes, 7, 8, 9 failures. The enormous 4W had been split into two for the fifth year, and my class was now just 15 strong. The less academic CSE exam was in its infancy in 1966, and John Sands recommended that certain pupils of borderline ability should be entered for both exams. My set was rated a little below grammar school average, with 8 being entered for 'O' level GCE, 3 of whom were a double entry. The other 7 were CSE only. Six passed the GCE (3 getting grade 4), and the two who didn't gained a CSE grade one. The rest got good CSE grades overall, including another grade one. For me this meant a good degree of pleasure and not a little relief.

The following year, 5S, whom I'd had now for four years, were my exam year class. I entered 23 of them for GCE and 10 for the CSE. All 23 passed, many with good or very good grades, and there were a few ones in the CSE.

Perhaps teachers (and indeed parents) can sometimes become obsessed with exam results; there are, after all, other components of a child's education — the personality and moral development, the possible sporting or artistic success among them. Qualifications, however, remain vital and teachers are always under pressure to 'bring home the bacon'; this was particularly true in the grammar school days. As far as I was concerned, I had something to prove with 5W and 5S, especially after the rather inauspicious start to my career. I could now feel that in the final count I had not done too badly with these classes.

By now I had developed sufficient technique to have good discipline in all the classes I had met since the end of my first year, and things had improved even with pupils I had had problems with earlier. I began to realise that if a teacher is confident enough to address a class in such a manner as presupposes that nothing will go wrong in the lesson, then nothing actually will. Certainly as far as the grammar school teaching went this worked well, and later with the majority in the comprehensive situation, too.

## Chapter Five

The set of boys I had in the fifth year in 1967-8 were as nice a bunch as you could wish to meet; some I had known for some time, others I had met more recently, but somehow they gelled together really well. Their keenness to speak French very much endeared them to me, and when their results came out in August they were very pleasing.

By 1969 the form that I had known since they were 2Y had become 5J. They were as eager and talented as ever, apart from one minor hiccup along the way. The exam that they took was the short-lived 'O' level alternative, which was more difficult than the orthodox 'O' level, containing set books which the students had to discuss in the oral exam.

We started one of the books towards the end of the fourth year, and as the year ground into July, I continued driving them hard, insensitive, I can now see all too clearly, to their fatigue. I know now that pupils, like teachers, can tire as the year nears its end, especially after a whole series of exams, and although they have to be kept going in some way, there are easier or less formal tasks they should be set. In 1968, though, as a still quite young teacher desperate to do well with his first top set, I had failed to understand this. And then, one lesson in mid-July, they went on strike. I began the lesson with enthusiasm, throwing out a question on the book, a World War II adventure story. No hand went up to answer it— a rare occurrence in any form at EPGS, let alone my star performers. I ended up answering my own question. A second question: no response. A third: same story. In the end I gave up and we did something else. The following September, however, they came out of the traps with all their usual élan and gave me a great run, right through to the early summer and the orals. These proved a testing time; I had two appalling migraines during the recordings (which I dreaded a repeat of every summer for the rest of my career, but which did not actually happen again) and one of the most gifted lads in the form became so nervous that he could hardly utter a word, failing totally to do himself justice. In later years I would know better how to cope with an over-stressed candidate; a joke, no matter how stupid, can work wonders. The written papers came and went; an anxious summer waiting for the results ensued.

In the meantime 5L, my own form, had taken their exams and left. On their last day they had put up a roll of paper on the wall with "General Gordon's Army" written at the top and all their names signed underneath. They gave me a farewell gift of wine and a very special book. This was a school exercise book filled with a collage of comments I had written on their French books over the years. I couldn't believe that they had gone to such trouble! There were dozens of remarks, over pages and pages:

"It is inexcusable that you do not know ... ."
"spoiled by careless errors."
"Does not make sense!"
"Writing just not good enough!"
"Think more carefully."
"How can the gender MIRACULOUSLY change?"
"Fool!"
"your spelling is digusting!", with their all too justified comment

alongside— "may we suggest an 's' in disgusting?" Oh dear!
"... obviously not been checked."
"unattractive to mark."
"don't waste space."
"As careless as ever."
"No such word!"
"See me."
"unfinished"
"not good."
"disappointing"
"What on earth ... ?"
"use a ruler"
"Care!"
"Why are there two holes in this book?"
"Aïe!!!"

This large number of unfavourable comments may make it appear that they were quite poor at French. This was not so; they could just as easily have compiled a book full of 'excellent', 'très bien', 'commendable', 'well tried' and so on. But 32 boys contributing from several years' work made a compilation of critical comments fairly easy. Looking back now, I can see that some of my remarks were over the top, but it was all part of the driving hard for results. The book, I feel, was compiled with affection; I treasure it accordingly.

I had taught another fifth year set in 1968-9, made up of boys from 5L and 5P. Officially it was set three. In fact I had put pressure on John Sands to let me have this set, since it contained a lot of my form. This meant I was teaching sets one and three. John Wolfenden very unselfishly agreed to take a lower set to enable this to happen. In all, therefore, I taught 65 fifth year pupils that year.

One Thursday morning late in August I drove into school trembling with nervousness, as I had done the three previous years, and as I have done ever since. Numerous toilet visits before leaving the house ... hardly able to eat any breakfast. I liked all 65 lads I had taught, and most of them I had known for years. For myself as a young professional I wanted to prove myself once and for all. I'd done reasonably well with sets 2 or 3 in previous years, but now, with my first top set expectations would be high from all the parents concerned and, of course, from the Headmaster and John Sands.

There were 10 grade ones in 5J, 8 grade twos; all had passed, all except one very comfortably. In set three, all those entered for 'O' level had passed, of the rest all bar two had a CSE grade one. All the hard work, the endless driving in class, the heaps of marking had been worth it. All the concern, the anxiety that had been at times sickening, had been unnecessary. I did not see Mr Hedges that morning; he must have come into school later. John Sands had been away on holiday when the results came out, but received a phone call from the Head upon his return.

"Congratulations on the French results, John! You've done it again!"

The Head had forgotten that it was not John himself who had taken the top set this year.

"They're not mine, they're Gordon's," explained John.

When John recounted this to me a few days later when we returned to school for the new year, I felt I was standing on Everest.

Early in 1969 John Sands had mooted the possibility of my taking a share in the 'A' level teaching the following September. He had in mind some language work with the lower sixth. This class would be made up mainly of boys from 5J, whom I knew very well; the move would enable me to continue teaching Ray Robinson and Kit Thorne (the two brightest stars in the class), among others and would be good for my career. Yet I hesitated. Was I up to it? I was concerned that I only had a General Degree, and that I hadn't spent a year in France.

It was Wesley Dixon, my best friend from Crewe Grammar, who had since taught the sixth form for French and German in Crewe, Nantwich and Rochdale who urged me not to miss the opportunity and convinced me that I was well up to the demands of 'A' level French teaching. I will be eternally grateful to Wes for this; sixth form teaching became one of the highlights of my week, stimulating and rewarding.

John wanted me to take the following year's lower sixth, whom I didn't know at all, for literature. Again I hesitated, well aware that literature had not been my forte at Crewe or Sheffield. Again Wes encouraged me, again I accepted.

I spent a lot of the 1970 summer holidays preparing the set books, the Molière play *Le Misanthrope* and Prévost's novel *Manon Lescaut*. I knew I was not God's gift to literature; I was determined to make a success of it by dint of very thorough preparation. I made copious notes, visiting libraries, buying books on the works, doing everything possible to hide any weaknesses of my own and to be able to cover the texts effectively.

The class was a good one; some in it were excellent. I think I did a reasonable job; another new vista had opened up for me. I felt happy in the school and pleased with what I was doing. The days of my disastrous beginning seemed ages ago.

## Chapter Six

At Ellesmere Port Boys' Grammar School the timetable allowed any sport-minded member of staff to have a couple of periods of games, which came as a welcome break from the academic work of the rest of the week. This also offered the opportunity to see another side to the pupils. I invariably found great pleasure in seeing someone who may not have been brilliant at French revealing great talent on, say, the football field.

In the summer term of my first year I was keen to help with cricket. I took a few practices with the first eleven and umpired several games. Peter Murphy, who was in charge of cricket, organised regular fixtures for several EPGS teams; he was therefore very dependent on staff volunteering to offer their umpiring services. In those days any staff who knew anything at all about cricket would be expected to sign up for at least one Saturday game during the season. Occasionally, even teachers with a considerably restricted knowledge of the game had to be roped in. Dave Ingram, for example, confessed to me that he really had no idea about how to give the batsman his guard; he did not realise that when a batsman asks for "one", he means a leg stump guard, and when he requests "two", he means middle and leg. Dave was under the impression that the off stump was "one" and middle stump was "two." No doubt he had more than his share of LBWs to give!

In truth EPGS was for the most part a fairly average school as far as cricket was concerned, but in the sixties we did help several very useful players to develop their talent. Ken Gerrard was a commanding, even arrogant batsman who thumped a memorable century against Helsby when I was umpiring; he, Jimmy Beahon, Phil Griffiths and Les Aston went on to enjoy success at a good level of club cricket. Of those who started in the sixties, though, Chris Fleet achieved most. At EPGS he was a very shrewd first eleven captain and batted with cultured aggression. He later made over 500 appearances for Chester Boughton Hall in the Liverpool Competition (equivalent to Minor Counties standard), captaining the 1st XI for twelve years and becoming the second highest run scorer in the club's history.

By the 1970s I was master in charge of cricket myself. It was in the spring of 1970 when I saw in action for the first time the boy who was to become the greatest cricketer our school had seen or, indeed, has seen since, a boy who was to bring us unprecedented glory.

A chilly April day, rain in the air, a fresh wind howling around the school field, conditions not all that conducive to honing the arts of the summer game. I walked out onto the practice area with Ian Roberts, one of the pool of players in our under thirteens, for the first weekly session of the season. Ian told me with enthusiasm of a new boy, who had the reputation of being very good at cricket, and who was very keen to come along.

The new boy's name was Richard Williams, recently arrived in the area from North Wales. He was short, stockily built, looking very strong in the forearms. Despite the unfavourable conditions, the impression that he made was extremely good. He stroked the ball around elegantly but with a power that belied his age. He could bowl, too, medium fast, accurate and with movement, and his fielding was excellent. Indeed, he could throw the ball further and with more precision than anyone I've seen on that field. Clearly already well-coached (by his father, I discovered) and full of fervour, he seemed a godsend for our team.

And so it proved. Against a local school Richard and Jeff Fleet (brother of Chris) scored 150 in 20 overs, carting the bowling all over the field. Richard then proceeded to shatter the opposition's batting with what they found to be unplayable bowling. The under 13s won eight out of nine fixtures, being robbed by rain of a ninth victory. Richard had three fifties, Jeff Fleet two.

The following season Richard was made captain of our under fourteen side, which we entered for the Esso Trophy, a competition open to all third year sides in Cheshire. He was so good, though, that he made several appearances for the under fifteens, too; further, he played for the Christleton first eleven in the Cheshire Cricket League. These games were on a Saturday afternoon, so he often played two games on the same day. He was physically strong enough to take this, however, and became the youngest player to score a century for Christleton when he was just fourteen.

At this age, none the less, there was a touch of the impetuous, the impatient about his batting which caused him to get out cheaply a few times. The under fourteens, however, progressed well in the Esso Trophy, beating Stanney, St Hugh's, Chester City Grammar and Calday. Richard took wickets galore, and in the Calday game hit 39 not out of the 45 we needed for victory.

The highlight of the season, however, was still to come. In the semi-final we were drawn against the prestigious Birkenhead School; EPGS had never registered a win against a school of such a reputation. My report from the 1971 school magazine tells what happened:

> "Starting decidedly second favourites against Birkenhead School, rated by most to be West Cheshire's best cricketing academy, we could but hope for at least a respectable performance from Williams' side. What we went on to witness surpassed our wildest dreams. The captain put up a fine exhibition of controlled, attacking medium-fast bowling, taking 7-22 when our opponents batted first, and Billy Allan bowled very economically at the other end. Williams and Lewis both contributed fine run-outs, and Birkenhead could manage no more than 54. Half an hour later, however, it seemed that even this modest total would be sufficient to beat us, with our score 13-4, and Williams among those back in the pavilion. Jeff Fleet, though, had other ideas. Proving his ability against spin bowling, he hit a fighting if occasionally risky 41 not out to see us through to victory."

Two memories particularly stand out from what was a high point in EPGS' cricket history. Richard, swinging out against the spin, spooned a high catch which was dropped. When he was at the bowler's end where I was umpiring, I said to him fiercely (and quite unprofessionally) under my breath:

"Don't do that again!"

A few minutes later he repeated his folly and this time, of course, he was caught. Once Richard had gone, I was very afraid we would collapse, but Jeff Fleet, to his eternal credit, did us proud. However, I was far from impressed by the ungracious manner in which the Birkenhead member of staff took the defeat.

"Your chap (meaning Jeff) was hitting across the line the whole time, you know. Damned lucky!"

*Richard Williams in action for Northamptonshire*

Maybe, but the scorebook had recorded irrefutably: "EPGS won by 4 wickets."

Alas, we did not win the Esso Trophy. In the final against Altrincham Grammar, Richard was dismissed for a low score and Jeff for nought. We lost by 6 wickets, Altrincham owing much to their star performer — Paul Allott, later to play for Lancashire and England.

The all-Cheshire competition at under fifteen level is the Dewes Cup, and in 1971 we reached the final for the first time. Once again, however, Altrincham stood in our way. They made 140-6, we could only manage 120, and had to be content to take home the Dewes Shield rather than the cup.

Revenge, however, was never sweeter than in 1972. The same two rivals made it through to the final again, with another Williams-Allott battle in prospect. Williams and Allan bowled superbly for us, taking five wickets apiece, and we dismissed Altrincham for 82. I was still far from confident. Jeff Fleet had by now left the school and I knew that if Richard failed we would have little chance. By now, though, his batting had developed; no chancy shots, no hitting against the spin. He batted with a maturity beyond his years. When we reached our victory target of 83 with only 3 wickets down, Richard Williams was 62 not out.

When Richard left school he signed on for Northamptonshire County Cricket Club and played for them for over twenty seasons until a knee injury forced his retirement. He never quite achieved full international recognition, although he did play for Young England and toured Sharjah with the MCC. At his peak he was being touted as an England possible by many pundits, among them Christopher Martin-Jenkins and Richie Benaud. By now Richard was bowling leg-spin rather than medium-fast, and it was said at this time that he turned the ball more than any other spinner in the country. Highlights of his professional career included a fine century against the West Indies, whose attack included Michael Holding, a career-best 175 not out against Leicestershire, and performing the hat-trick against Gloucestershire.

As a youngster I was not particularly gifted at soccer, but was football crazy, and have more or less remained so ever since. My first experience of the professional game was in the autumn of 1949; my father and I in the stand at Gresty Road — Crewe Alexandra 3, Hull City 1. Just an ordinary third division encounter, I suppose, but to me there was something magical about the whole thing: the white goal posts with the neatly-arranged netting, the greenness of the turf, the colours of the players' kits— the bold red and white of the Alex, the gold and black of Hull; then the enthralling battle that ensued. I was captured for life.

It was John Chiverrell, a colleague from the Geography Department and master in charge of football from the mid-sixties onwards, who persuaded me to take on the running of a football team at EPGS. I hesitated, wondering if I had the ability to coach a side well, but finally agreed. 'Chiv' was a big help, coming along to my practice sessions and giving tactical talks to the lads. They proved an above average team, winning more than they lost, and I started to enjoy this new dimension to my school life, recalling now with affection the chilly Saturday mornings spent refereeing or cheering the lads on at away fixtures. Refereeing could bring its problems, however. One of these was that you rarely had linesmen, as a result of which it was sometimes very difficult to judge offsides. I think that most spectators appreciated this, but there was the occasional dissenting voice from the touchline. What I really objected to was when this voice came from the member of staff from the opposing school. A certain teacher from a local school was a notable pain in the posterior in this respect.

There was one Saturday morning which Chiv might prefer to forget. I was waiting outside school with two full soccer teams, and the time at which Chiv had said he'd be there with the key came and went. Eventually we saw his car coming along the road by the school, then turning into the school drive, but it was not alone. Right behind it, lights flashing, siren blaring, came a police car. Chiv, it seemed, had been speeding, and having arrived at the school front door, had to face the indignation of the law. It transpired that Chiv had overslept and was doing 48 mph through Whitby (speed limit 30) when the cops saw him. Twenty-odd kids had plenty to tell their parents that Saturday lunchtime.

I ran my first soccer team for three years, then another for four years between 1970-1 and 1973-4. This second side contained even more good talent and we reached the semi-finals of the Emberton Cup (U15 trophy for the whole of Cheshire) in 1974. I trained them extremely hard for the game, calling them in for extra sessions. Our opponents, however, Sutton School, won 8-3; we were simply outclassed by a team that went on to win the trophy.

A boy from my very special form of 1964–9 was one of the best footballers our school produced. This was Paul Jones. Along with Barry Siddall, Neil Whatmore and Paul Holding, Paul was signed on for Bolton Wanderers following the visit of a scout to the school one Saturday morning. I had seen Paul play several times, but not as many as I would have liked. This restriction was imposed by the fact that I had my own team to run on Saturdays. I knew Paul better as a cricketer; he was a fine all-rounder in the side I had charge of, a flowing, attacking batsman, a very gifted bowler, of medium pace, one of that rare breed able to drop the ball onto a sixpence almost every time, and a fine fielder with a strong, accurate throw. Paul was also a fine athlete and rugby player. Academically he had a good attitude and held his own.

Paul had played centre-forward in his early days as a footballer, but by the third year he was a stylish, commanding central defender who read the game well, a fine stopper, classy on the ball which he distributed well; he looked to have a very promising future. In fact he went on to play 405 times for Bolton, scoring 43 goals, mainly with his head from corners or set-pieces. England manager Don Revie selected Paul in his squad for a full international match, but unfortunately Paul did not actually get to play for his country.

Paul Holding unhappily fell by the wayside due to injury, but the Bolton side of the seventies regularly contained three old EPGS pupils, with Barry Siddall and Neil Whatmore in the team as well as Paul Jones.

Barry Siddall, strong as an ox at an early age, was an excellent all-round sportsman. He shone at cricket, rugby and athletics (triple-jump and hurdles) as well as soccer. Barry was made to do rugby for his first two years at EPGS, but finally became our regular goalkeeper in year three, taking over the spot from none other than Richard (Rick) Parry, who became another famous old boy when appointed Chief Executive of the Premier League and later of Liverpool F.C. To any opposing attacker, Siddall must have been an awesome sight, seeming almost to fill the goal;

*EPGS First year soccer team, 1967.*
*Back row (L–R): Michael Whittaker, Chris Fleet, Neil Whatmore, Michael Mawdsley, Keith Hughes, Paul Bedward. Front row: David Jarvis, Terry Ashcroft, Craig McAteer, Richard Sheen, Colin Hunt.*

he also had tremendous agility and very rapid reactions. He was without doubt the best goalkeeper in the school's history to date.

Barry's mother became a familiar figure at all the school games where he was playing. She cheered on the lads with great enthusiasm and invariably brought with her enough sustenance for the whole team to enjoy half-time refreshments. She gained great satisfaction from her son's success, both at school and later in the professional game. Barry made 158 appearances for Bolton, then went on to play for a large number of clubs, including Tranmere Rovers, Blackpool, Sunderland, Carlisle, Stockport, Port Vale and Chester.

Some three years before I left Whitby, I was delighted to meet up again with Barry. He was playing for Chester at the time, but was unable to train at one point through injury. I was honoured that he came back to his old school specifically to see me. Chatting over old and present times was a great pleasure.

Apart from Mrs Siddall, another parent who gave fine support was Ron Fleet, father of Chris and Jeff. Chris played soccer as well as cricket for the school, and when he was in the first year Ron arranged with Chester F.C. player-manager Peter Hauser for the whole squad to train at the club one morning, meeting the players and being shown around. What a thrill for football-mad youngsters! Ron knew football and cricket very well, and gave valuable advice to staff and pupils.

Neil Whatmore, known as 'Bobby', was another versatile sportsman, talented at cricket, rugby, soccer and athletics. Neil was a prolific goal scorer, the finest attacking player the school ever knew. He had a natural instinct for being in the right place when the ball arrived; he was two-footed; he was a good header of the ball; he had speed.

I recall refereeing at the King's School, Chester, one Saturday morning, when Neil scored six. At half-time, with the score 9-0 in our favour, I could hear the rather loud, plummy voice of the King's School teacher addressing his team:

"Look here, you chaps, I know we're going to lose this one, but by golly, we're going to go down fighting!"

The final score was 18-0. Neil and Mike Mawdsley simply ran riot!

Neil became a great favourite with the crowd at Burnden Park, making 338 appearances for Bolton and scoring 121 goals. Further success at Birmingham followed before he ended his career at Mansfield Town.

The team in which Whatmore, Holding and Siddall played (Paul Jones was two years older) was the most successful ever at the school. Despite the calls of the rugby club, which weakened the soccer team for the first two years, this side only ever lost one game. In the fourth year they won the two-legged Emberton Cup Final by an aggregate of 11-0!

Michael Wright, who was in the first year when the school opened in 1959, was the first EPGS pupil to become a professional footballer. A speedy full-back, he played several seasons at Aston Villa. In more recent years, Phil Hardy (Wrexham and Republic of Ireland U21s) and Dave Challinor (Tranmere Rovers) have made the grade. Challinor, in fact, holds the record for the longest throw-in in British football. Rob Jones, however, has proved the only old boy so far to play at full international level. I taught Rob French when he was in year one; he was a pleasant lad, but, alas, possessed of only modest ability. In athletics, though, he was outstanding, both in sprints and long-distance races. As far as soccer was concerned, as a youngster he would practise for hours honing skills that seemed to a large extent inborn in him. He was quick, determined in the tackle, and a classy distributor of the ball. Further, his athletic prowess and willingness to train made him a very fit footballer. From school he joined Dario Gradi's Crewe Alexandra, making 90 appearances for them before transferring to Liverpool, where he became the regular right-back, and gained full international recognition for England.

Another fine all-round sportsman from the school was Steve Marland, who represented his county at under sixteen level in football, rugby and athletics, and was an England under 18 soccer international. Steve won a sports scholarship to the University of Washington DC.

It was in 1967 that John Young, the Head of PE, had the idea of having a whole afternoon of cross-country running. There were to be three races, one for juniors (years 1-2), one intermediate (3-4) and one senior (5-6), run over the Shell field (situated across the road from the school) and the adjacent Stanney Woods. Members of staff were to be posted all over the course to prevent cheating. When they heard of the projected senior race, some of the sixth form were incensed and objected strongly, giving the excuse that they no longer had running kit and therefore couldn't participate.

"Look," said John, "I don't care what you run in, as long as you run!"

They took John at his word. When the sixth form boys emerged from the changing rooms, they were all wearing women's clothes!

With John Young the driving force behind rugby, Ellesmere Port

Grammar was always a strong school in that sport, able to take on the county's best with a good measure of success. John Bassnett became an England U21 rugby union international, then went on to rugby league stardom with Widnes and Leeds. Denis Morgan was an English Schools international, then played for New Brighton R.U.F.C.

But John Jackson Page, always known as "Jacko", has proved the only rugby player from the school to date to achieve full international status. Prematurely bald due, apparently, to a dragon fly's sting when he was at primary school, Page was a superb handler of a rugby ball who became a Cambridge rugby blue twice and played for England in 1970-1 in all four games in the Five Nations Tournament. Further, in 1974-5, reports indicate that he played a leading role in England's win over Scotland.

Jane Parry was an outstanding sprinter in the school in the late seventies and early eighties, becoming one of the top women's 100 metres runners in the country, almost reaching Olympic standard.

In hockey the extremely skilful, strong and determined Michael Perry played for the English Schools' under nineteens.

By 1974 I had been involved with cricket, football, hockey and table tennis and had enjoyed hundreds of hours of fulfilment in sporting activities. The advent of comprehensivisation, however, brought with it a rule that no one without a sports education qualification could take games lessons. This represented the end of an era.

# Chapter Seven

Characters. The school has certainly seen its share of them on the staff over the years. Many were brilliant teachers, some tried hard but could not quite cope, a few, regrettably, must be classed as absolute charlatans.

One of the biggest charlatans of the lot was a cravat-sporting maths teacher who boasted to me that he never marked any books, and invented figures for his markbook when a parents' evening loomed. He also developed the technique of awarding pupils ludicrously inflated grades on their reports, so that the following year, when some unfortunate other teacher took them over and gave them an honest rating, a parent might say:

"But he had a much better grade with that nice Mr ..."

A certain man of the cloth who had been a padre in the Far East, where, after stepping on a mine, he had acquired an unfortunate limp which would stay with him for the rest of his days, came to teach at the school. His timetable was mostly R.E., of course, and somehow or other he managed to get away with writing 'Life of Christ' (what they were studying) on everyone's report rather than a comment on the child's ability. He was one of the first (there would be others later) to realise that if a teacher walks around everywhere brandishing a clipboard, then he or she creates the illusion of being extremely busy and efficient. Our padre was neither.

At this time some of the staff were trying to solve a mystery. One of their number, but no one knew exactly who, was using the staff toilet very early in the morning and leaving the cloakroom in which it was situated stinking to high heaven; the result was that when teachers came in to hang up their outer coats they were met by a stench that had them clasping their handkerchiefs to their noses until they could escape it. A notice was duly pinned to the staffroom door:

"Who is the Phantom Sulphide?"

Then one morning the mystery was solved. A teacher going in very early himself for some reason was met by the offending pong as he entered the cloakroom, whereupon the chain was pulled and out came the padre!

The padre also helped with rowing, on one occasion being in a boat with the pupils when it capsized. Leaving the boys floundering in the River Dee, he quickly made sure of his own safety! It seems that he was more than fond of rendering homage to Bacchus; he would often adjourn to the Boathouse Inn long before the rowing session was supposed to end, and, when he finally left the school, the successor to his room found the stockroom liberally strewn with empty beer bottles!

In July 1999, a large, dusty volume was discovered in an old cupboard of the admin block in Whitby High School. It was Kenneth Hedges' staff register. Of the padre, the Head had written:

"Left to take up a curacy somewhere in Worcestershire, leaving behind unpaid bills and an unsavoury reputation."

A second reverend tried very hard, but found the Ellesmere Port boys much less receptive to R.E. and history as he taught them than the African children he had formerly had dealings with. I recall one occasion when he was teaching a third year in the classroom under mine and the class were making a fearful row.

"Right!" he shouted in utter desperation, "You're going to be quiet for fifteen seconds! Fifteen seconds, do you hear? I'm going to start counting. One ..."

The class fell into absolute silence. "... two ... three ... ." Still silence. On he counted. "... thirteen ... fourteen ... fifteen," to be followed by the most almighty explosion of din imaginable, which rendered his whole exercise futile!

He was extremely well-spoken, pronouncing "ruler" as "rula", which, again in the room under mine, I could hear quite clearly.

"Take your rula!", he ordered, to be followed by the whole class chanting "Rula! Rula! Rula!"

Eventually he suffered a nervous breakdown, and underwent electric convulsive therapy. This may have done him some good, but unfortunately had the effect of wiping out all the children's names from his memory!

A third man of God, who had actually participated in the battle of Arnhem and sustained a dent in his skull for his pains, found it equally difficult to relate to our boys. He talked extremely far-back and had a public school background. He told me that he had found running a parish in Ireland far easier than teaching at EPGS.

There was a boy in one of his classes who rejoiced in the name of Finch Cadwallader. One lesson this boy was playing up the reverend, who screamed at him:

"Good name for you, Cadwallader, because you are a cad!"

The class exploded.

On another occasion he was trying to belabour a boy who, to take cover, hid under a desk.

"Come out from under there, Johnson, and let me hit you!", yelled the reverend.

On Friday afternoons he had a class which had placed religious education well down on their list of priorities. In the end the reverend gave up, and, in total disregard of those trying to teach in adjoining rooms, played his boys jazz records at full blast!

Outside the reverend's classroom was a fire hose, normally, of course, kept rolled up in its metal holder on the wall. One day, however, a certain 4S, whilst awaiting the reverend's arrival, took the hose out of its holder then smuggled it into the room when their teacher eventually came along. By a point about half way through the lesson, the reverend had filled two boards with the notes the pupils had to write down and was standing at the front of the room. Suddenly the fire hose, aimed straight at the reverend, was turned on, spurting its jet of water all over him and obliterating totally the notes on the board behind him. He flew into a rage, lashing out at everyone who happened to be sitting in the first few rows, smacking heads galore, as the water gushed all over the place. In the end the hose was turned off and the reverend ceased berating his pupils. He decided that the whole class would be put on detention, and duly went into his stockroom to get the requisite number of slips. A mistake! One of the boys closed the door and turned the key. Cries of "Let me out, you bounders!" were cheerfully ignored. Then, just before the end of the lesson, the reverend heard the key turn in the lock. He opened the door and saw the class sitting there quietly. He made his way slowly to the front table, then sat down and, to the class' horror, began sobbing loudly. They hadn't wanted this— just a lark, that was all. And so, in their total defeat of the reverend they found only appalling remorse.

Basil Taffs was appointed laboratory steward in the early grammar school days, but, due to a teacher shortage, became, at the unlikely age of 62, a science master. The pupils, however, soon got wise to Basil's rather less than authoritarian approach and became increasingly boisterous in his lessons. Basil developed the habit of crashing the base of a bunsen burner down on the table in vain attempts to establish silence in the room, with the result that even today the wooden surface of the table where Basil had stood remains deeply pitted. Basil also made the mistake of setting hundreds and hundreds of lines (doubling every time the punishment was not handed in) to offending students, with the result that most transgressors never did do the lines. And when a few did, Basil never read them. On one occasion it was pointed out to him that a pupil, in the middle of the lines Basil had set, had written:
"O Basilio, o Basilio, I fart on thee, Basilio," which Basil had failed to notice.
Occasionally Basil would set an essay as a punishment as a change from

lines. A boy called Thompson received the order to write a two-page essay entitled "Hydrochloric Acid" for fooling around in the lab. Several lessons later, Thompson having repeatedly failed to produce it, Basil announced:

"Right, Thompson, you will now write me a 64-page essay on hydrochloric acid!"

"Sir," offered Thompson, "will it be all right if I write a two-page essay on concentrated hydrochloric acid?"

Basil would sometimes stumble through his words while attempting to explain a topic to his less than attentive class, and his experiments were not always well conducted. One day he was supposed to be producing oxygen by heating together two chemicals— potassium chlorate (a white powder) and manganese dioxide (a black powder). Basil began to heat the test tube with a bunsen burner, anticipating the appearance of bubbles after a few minutes. No bubbles. After half an hour, with still no bubbles in view, the bottom of the test tube having burned away, the class was in uproar, laughing, mocking. Basil's choice of the wrong black powder had wrecked his lesson.

A short time later, the shortage having passed, Basil became once again lab steward, his line-setting, bunsen burner-banging days seemingly over for ever. But no! Basil moved on, not to be a lab steward somewhere else, but, to the stupefaction of everyone at Ellesmere Port Grammar School, to a Deputy Headship at a small private school near Chester.

Godfrey Lloyd, formerly cadet of the year at Cranwell, no less, was among the most eccentric of the early teachers at the school. For example, rather than sit at a table to mark a pile of books like everyone else did, he would mark thirty-odd pieces of work whilst standing against a set of staff room lockers. And whereas everyone else took off their gowns (which we taught in in those days) before making their way to their transport home, Godfrey did not. He took on the appearance of a latter-day Dracula when seen riding his bike through Ellesmere Port with his gown billowing out in the breeze behind him. On rainy days, however, Godfrey, bedecked in broad yellow sou'wester, enormous yellow cape and black wellington boots, rode as if he was heading for some remote outpost in Labrador or Lapland. On one occasion, Godfrey, in flagrant disobedience of the laws concerning the riding of a bicycle, even rode his vehicle carrying his cello to a school concert.

Godfrey, alas, did not have good discipline as a teacher. He would sometimes stand in front of a class with his eyes closed or with a look of utter despair on his face. Maths master Athol Barrington tells me that one lesson he had the misfortune to be teaching next door to Godfrey, from whose class a great clamour was emanating. Athol left his own class working quietly to go and investigate, and found the hapless Godders standing outside the room.

"I'm not going in there till they're quiet," he announced, whereupon Athol opened Godfrey's door. Stepping inside, he was hit by a board duster dropping down from the ledge above, which spattered him liberally with its chalk dust. The class fell into a sudden silence, and a girl on the front row burst into tears.

"I'm so sorry," she lamented, "it wasn't meant for you, Mr Barrington, it was meant for Mr Lloyd".

For all his eccentricities, none the less, I am told that Godfrey was a conscientious most enthusiastic form tutor, finding imaginative activities for his pupils in all his form periods.

At the end of his third term, however, he was informed that he had not passed his probationary year. There would be no happy ending for Godfrey at EPGS.

A certain science teacher from the sixties could also be somewhat eccentric in his behaviour. He was the only teacher who walked all the way from Chester to school (about seven miles), and he was once caught weight-training in the gym at midnight, a passer-by having alerted the police, thinking the school had been broken into. This teacher had his own set of school keys, which, since he had a habit of losing things, he elected to bury on the school grounds. The problem was, though, that when he next needed the keys, he had forgotten where he had buried them!

One day, to demonstrate gravity to his physics class, he climbed up onto the school roof and was proceeding, leaning over the edge of the roof, to drop weights down from it. An alarmed resident in a house across the road from the school, however, rang up the school office convinced that a man was about to throw himself from the roof!

This teacher, in his early twenties, rather lacked authority in the classroom and frequently sent out pupils. Sometimes he would have five or six at once in the corridor, and the noise coming from outside surpassed that in the room itself. A regular offender was a girl called M..., who was often expulsed and yelled at quite alarmingly. After he had left, this teacher, recently married, popped into school to show off his bride to his former pupils. Their state of shock was palpable; 'Sir' had married M... !

A geography teacher, referred to by some of the pupils as "a lazy bastard", and said by some of the staff to have two speeds around the school— "dead slow" and "stop", used regularly to nip off ten minutes early in the afternoon. He would say to his class around 3.50:

"I've got to make a phone call" or "I've got to see the Head," followed by "If I'm not back by four o'clock you can go."

They well knew, of course, that he would not be back. By the time the bell went, having exited through the staff room window a few minutes before (to avoid being seen by the Head), he was well on his way to Chester!

On one occasion, however, this same teacher, being free last lesson on this particular day, had become totally absorbed in relating to some colleagues his exploits on the Matterhorn. To his horror, he suddenly realised that the bell had gone. The story quickly ended, he opened the staff room window, backward-rolled out of it and made his way rather hastily for him to the car park.

Dave Williamson was a maths teacher in the school's early days. To say he was unconventional would be an understatement. When asked once by the Headmaster at a break-time staff meeting what class he had next lesson, he replied:

"I've no idea. Whoever comes through the door, I teach them!"

Once at an informal meeting between the governors and the staff, one of the former asked Dave politely:

"And what do you think of the school?"

Dave was never the man to give a standard reply.

"It's warm, it's dry. The roof doesn't leak, I suppose," was his blasé response.

His unorthodox ways made it difficult for people to deal with him at times. Once, when feeling at a low ebb, he said to a rather perplexed Headmaster:

"Hey, Mr Hedges, I'm fed up! Will you sack me?"

When Dave first came to the school, everyone could see that he walked with a limp, but it was not at first realised that he had a wooden section to his right leg. Introducing himself to one of his classes, he announced:

"If anyone annoys me, this is what will happen to you."

Then, raising a compass point high into the air, he plunged it viciously into his own (wooden!) leg. One boy fainted. The rest sat in ashen-faced terror.

Dave had in fact lost half his leg in a motor-cycling accident in the late thirties. However, whenever he got into conversation with a German assistant, he would maliciously point to the wood and say:

"You buggers did this in the war!"

He was not averse to clipping the odd ear, but for the most part his bark was worse than his bite. He once called a boy who had annoyed him down to the front and held his own finger and thumb slightly apart. He then told the boy to put his ear between them and jerk his head up and down as his punishment!

Dave was, without doubt, an effective teacher who got good results and he did have the ability to strike real fear into miscreants. Once Dave, on duty in the dining hall, slipped on some custard that had fallen onto the floor. The room became totally silent when everyone saw that Dave had crashed to the ground. Not a smirk, not a snigger. Without a word Dave heaved himself up and resumed his round professionally. Gradually the murmur of conversation returned. The episode was over.

Conversely Dave could be very unprofessional at times. Keith Muscott tells of an occasion when he was teaching in Dave's room for a period when Dave was free. Suddenly the door opened, and there stood Dave. He hoisted himself up onto the upper part of the door frame, and started performing pull-ups, with a mischievous glint in his eye and his pipe in his mouth! Keith, a young teacher at the time, and still to become established in the school, had to endure stoically the sabotaging of his lesson.

Slim, debonair, invariably immaculately turned out (he taught in extremely expensive suits) and very susceptible to the charms of the opposite sex, Ian Ellis taught music in the grammar school between 1962 and 1967. He was a very talented pianist, performing Mozart's 23rd piano concerto with great success in the school hall, as a report at the time confirms:

> Delicate as filigree work in his technique and with consummate clarity of expression, the pianist held the audience entranced.

He had a fine tenor voice, too, singing the leads in *The Pirates of Penzance*, *The Mikado* and *Ruddigore*. During *The Mikado*, in which Ian was playing Nanki-Poo, John Sands, in the role of the pompous Poo-Bah, stomach-butted Ian as scripted, but, as not scripted, knocked him clean off the stage!

Ian developed the habit of starting his lessons by clapping his hands together and saying "Right!" to gain the class' attention. In one class that he taught, however, was a smart-arse called Wright. Every time Ian said "Right!", Wright would shout out "Yes, sir?"

Like most staff during the sixties, Ian was called upon to carry out sporting duties as part of his timetable. Most of us found ourselves involved with sports we were keen on, so how Ian was put down for cross-country, in which he had little interest, is not clear. The start of the course was in Dunkirk Lane, on the edge of Stanney Woods, just across the road from the school. Ian would drive his car down to the start, deign to get out of it to begin the race, then return to it to listen to music while the race took place. This, of course, led to all kinds of skiving on the part of some of the runners, who would disappear into the woods, sit around there for half an hour, then rejoin the race when the genuine contestants came past them again. But one day things went badly wrong. A boy fell during the race, injuring himself on some barbed wire, and when he emerged at the end he seemed to be streaming blood. He staggered towards Ian's car (which was invariably kept scrupulously clean), eventually collapsing over its bonnet. Ian bounded from the driver's seat with the words:

"Be careful, boy, you're getting blood on the car!!"— before seeing the boy safely to the school nurse.

Pupils would play the odd trick on Ian during his first year's teaching; most debutants, it seemed, were fair game! One lesson with a second year class Ian suddenly noticed that a boy who had been sitting at the front of the class had disappeared. It transpired that the boy, noticing the absence of the wooden lower back of Ian's piano, had clambered inside the instrument!

When Ian taught he was prone to flamboyant hand and arm gestures to get over his message. One day, with Ian completely carried away by his enthusiasm, his sweeping arm movement resulted in his knocking the spectacles of a boy on the front row clean off his nose and right over to the other side of the classroom!

Ian was one of the infamous seven of the 1964 staff meeting concerning the staff dating of sixth form girls.

"How ironic," he said to me recently, "that I was stopped from going out with a girl five years younger than myself and end up marrying one fifteen years younger!"

David Leedham had two spells of teaching history at EPGS/Whitby. He arrived in 1965, stayed nine years, then returned in 1985, teaching a further eight years until his retirement in 1993.

David invariably made a strong impression on all who came into contact with him. As a teacher he gave of himself unsparingly to his classes, usually finishing his day's work totally drained. His enthusiasm for history knew no bounds. Pupils have told me of his vivid accounts of battles and significant events of history, how he seemed to make everything come alive in front of their eyes. His artistic gifts were also well appreciated. One boy told me:

"Mr Leedham could knock out a brilliant cathedral on the board in a few seconds!"

But David had his opponents, too, people who objected to his rigorous demand for the highest standards of work and his insistence on the use of a fountain pen in the writing of notes and essays. Several parents complained that he was asking too much, but he would not give an inch.

"You're not doing your job properly if you're not getting parents complaining about you" was his rather far-out point of view. One such parent was a Mrs H, although her complaint was coloured by the fact that her daughter's fountain pen unhappily went missing. She expressed her wrath in her own rather disrespectful and somewhat less than literate style:

> Dear Leadham
> K........ has done her homework in Biro her fountain pen was stoled in school and nothing has been Done about it, I pay my Rate's so I do not see why I should carry on providing the school with fountain pens. all so the teacher learn's her, and the teacher should make an effert that there is no more stealing
> Mrs H

David once had a boy in one of his history sets called Leedham, and steadfastly refused to call the pupil by a name the same as his own.

"I shall call you Peters," he told the boy, who had no alternative but to accept his new appellation.

David found attaining 30 years of age a notably traumatic experience,

all the more so since he was convinced he looked much less than his years. Accordingly he asked one of his classes:
"How old do you think I look?"
"About 45, sir," replied one lad.

In his second spell at the school, David confined himself to the teaching of history, becoming Head of Department. In the sixties, however, he also helped run the rowing club, giving up every Saturday to do so, and made a speciality of taking assemblies. These were deliberately provocative, often extreme, but always sincerely and dynamically delivered. Unlike most assemblies, the pupils looked forward to the "D.L. Show". In one address, wishing to underline the essentially humble background of Jesus Christ, David referred to him as "this grotty Jew", causing a stir, no doubt to David's delight, through the whole school, incurring great anger in some more traditional quarters. Shortly after this, at the school cottage one weekend, a group of lads from my own form went around singing, to the tune of Ken Dodd's *Happiness*:

"Grottiness, grottiness, the greatest gift that I possess!"

In another assembly David emphasised that the freedom which the Gospels offered was for everyone, including, as he indicated the boys on the front row,

"the third former worrying himself sick about masturbation because he can't sufficiently break through the prudery that surrounds him to be able to talk about it."

More uproar! More outrage from the R.E. Department! Sadly, the following week's assembly, delivered by one of the traditionalists, addressed and condemned "self-abuse."

David saw Jesus as "the man who calls us to leave the thousand and one prisons that, scared of ourselves, we create for ourselves; the man who calls us into life and into more life; the man who proclaims freedom, freedom to be ourselves, freedom from the bondage of religion and false beliefs, freedom from inherited ideas and prejudices, freedom from the fear of others and the fear of ourselves."

Three decades on the scripts of David's orations have lost none of their significance and power; indeed, it is easy to see how far ahead of his time he was. There was a sensitivity underlying the extravagant delivery of these assemblies; they really did speak to and sympathise with the young people sitting and listening to them. The message was not just to the masturbators, but to:

"the boy who tries so hard but never makes it."

"the boy who is incredibly shy, locked in his own world as people and opportunities pass him by."

On yet another occasion, David, lifting his admittedly fraying gown high as he spoke, referred to it as "this tatty symbol of a not quite achieved academic glory."

More offence, more ire.

Perhaps David did go too far at times, perhaps he was too deliberately controversial, but he invariably brought out a response from staff and pupils alike and he certainly shook people out of their early morning torpor.

In his final year's teaching at Whitby, David taught a boy who developed the anti-social habit of farting loudly in people's lessons. David decided to solve the problem by sending him to the school nurse whom he had primed to administer a spoonful of the most revolting medicine to the boy, ostensibly to stop his passing wind. David also gave the boy an essay to write on the subject, which he failed to do, leaving David no alternative but to give him a detention instead. In a very roughly-hewn tour de force of indignation, the boy's mother laid down her feelings thus:

> Dear Mr Leedham,
> X will not be doing any detention, for not writing a essay on wind. I have never heard any rubbish in all my life. it is one of the natural body fuctions so to do. Do teachers write essays out when they break wind.
>   I think the nurse should go back to collage and learn more herself if a child holds the wind in he would be ill with stomach pains, surley this is obvious to yourself even.
>   Thanking you
>   Mrs ...
>   P.S. I am sure the Ellesmere Port Pioneer would love to here this pathtic story or even the daily papers. What would the headlines be? Boy gets detention for breaking wind, but teachers do it freely.

David retired from teaching at 50, following an inheritance from an aunt. In fact, in all he spent only 19 years in the classroom— 17 in Ellesmere Port, two in Colwyn Bay; however, during that time he made a terrific impact, showing immense energy. All the more ironical, therefore, that on his last day at Whitby an earnest and concerned-looking first former asked him:

"Will you be going into a nursing home now, sir?"

Allan Pemberton, from the Craft Department, tall, craggy, spiky-haired and muscular, must have seemed a mountain of a man to the pupils, who were all, without exception, terrified of him. So much so in the case of one small boy that when he saw 'Pembo' coming down the corridor towards him, he defecated on the spot. Pembo had highly individual methods of discipline. He insisted, when the boys lined up outside his room, that they stood exactly on the third tile out from the wall. One day a boy called Ingram was seen by Pembo standing on the fourth tile. He was summoned into the room, and told he would be dealt with. Pembo told the boy that when he (Pembo) banged on a bench, he (the boy) must scream out as if he was being hit. Two bangs followed, each accompanied by the requested scream. The boys outside started to laugh, realising, though they could see nothing, that their comrade was not really being hit. Pembo's black sense of humour, however, took over at this point and his third (not too hard) blow landed on the boy who, to the increased amusement of his classmates outside, this time let out a genuine cry of discomfort!

Pembo's humour could even border on the bizarre at times. One very hot day, as the boys toiled around the furnace, Pembo announced:

"Look, lads, I know you all must be boiling hot, and I've arranged for matron to make you a big jug of lemonade with lots of ice in it. It just needs picking up from the kitchen. Laidler, would you go and get it?"

But just as Laidler was going out, Pembo called him back:

"Sorry, Laidler, only joking!"

Pembo rigged up a bell in his desk, on the lid of which he placed a toy telephone. During the lesson he would make the bell ring, then pick up the phone and have a lengthy mock-conversation with the non-existent caller, while the class waited patiently for the supposed business to be concluded.

A boy called McCarthy had the misfortune to meet Pembo during the holidays on a beach in Wales. Back at school in September, Pembo taunted the boy by saying to the class:

"Guess who I saw picking up pretty little shells on the beach!"

It seems that Pembo ribbed this boy a fair amount. However, a tragedy in the boy's life was to change this. One day, after the boy had been absent, Pembo asked him why.

"My father died last week, sir," replied McCarthy.

From that moment Pembo became a different man, showing the boy consideration and affection, revealing the human side of his character which had lain hidden under the fearsome exterior and the weird humour. And if a boy showed a real interest in the work, Pembo would really put himself out for him. One ex-pupil told me how Pembo laboured with him on a piece of mahogany until the sweat poured from him.

Jack Thomas served 23 years at EPGS/Whitby, arriving in 1965. He had been an R.A.F. fighter pilot in the war, and had the misfortune to crash five aircraft (three Swordfish, two Harvards), but the good luck to survive the mishaps.

"I should have had the Iron Cross," he joked, " the Germans gave it to their pilots for wrecking five British aircraft!"

Jack had come to Ellesmere Port after seventeen years at the very tough Hamilton Secondary Modern School in Birkenhead, so the Ellesmere Port boys were comparatively easy to deal with after his previous place of work. Jack told me of one amusing incident at Hamilton when an art inspector walked into his lesson, announcing to the boys:

"I am very keen to see your work," whereupon thirty lads rushed forward with their still-wet paintings in their hands. In an attempt to avoid getting paint on his clothes as the paintings were proffered, he stepped backwards, knocking open the door of a stockroom from which several pots of paint fell on him, ruining his suit!

Art was Jack's principal teaching subject, but he became a leading figure in the school, being firstly a year-group head, then a timetabler of great skill, then careers master.

Jack had one 'A' level class at EPGS that he got on particularly well with, one that he could laugh and joke with without detriment to the work. Once he set them an essay to write on whatever German expressionist they wished to choose. As it happened, they all chose Helmut Schwenk. Jack was at first alarmed, since he had not heard of this artist, but as he read on into their essays he realised that there were conflicting details in them; it did not take him too long to comprehend that Helmut Schwenk was a figment of their collective imaginations! Going along with their joke, Jack brought out a bogus biography of Herr Schwenk and gave them all a copy!

Jack had to go into hospital for a while that year, and while he was recovering, in trooped the 'A' level set, waving banners with "Get well, Uncle Jack" written on them, and noisily announcing

"We've brought some of your favourite reading!" as they brandished garish horror comics for all the ward to see!

Jack loved his time at the school, so much so in fact that he taught until he was 64, a rarity in the latter days of the century.

## Chapter Eight

Ron Durdey was not only Head of History in the grammar school days; he devoted himself unstintingly to the production of the annual school play. He was uncompromising in his choice of works, these making enormous demands of the young actors concerned, especially those taking leading roles; however, Ron's patient dedication and insightful interpretation of the texts brought out the best in his young protégés and performances invariably attained high standards. Most of the plays selected were of a serious nature, reflecting Ron's own considerable gravitas, but Gogol's *The Government Inspector* was one of his lighter productions, very successfully brought off.

Chris White played the leading part of the mayor in this presentation, and during his career at EPGS proved himself an immensely talented and versatile young actor. He also had a wonderful sense of fun, as a revue I saw him in confirmed. When heavily into Shakespeare he went around the school limping and stooping, with contorted facial features, in an impressive Richard III take-off, declaiming quotes such as "A horse, a horse! My kingdom for a horse!" and "Now is the winter of our discontent ..." down the corridors. Chris went on to train at the Bristol Old Vic, later, after taking on the name Chris Selby, becoming assistant director at the Theatre Clwyd. He also had the honour of producing Ibsen plays in Norway, the land of the great dramatist's birth, and I understand that he spent some time in Hollywood, where he was involved in TV production.

Peter Cann was another bright talent around this time, both in sport (especially rowing) and drama. He took on ultra-demanding roles in *Billy Budd* and *An Enemy of the People*. Of the actresses brought over from the girls' school, Sandra Lewis was especially good. Sandra trained for the theatre later and became involved in Theatre in Education.

*Ian Hope as King Lear*

Ian Hope took on some monumental roles with outstanding success over a wide range of plays. In Ibsen's *Pillars of the Community* he played Karsten Bernich and had the very challenging title role in *King Lear*, fully justifying Ron Durdey's faith in him. Ian was Head Boy of the school for the year 1964-5 and a fine academic, gaining a place at Southampton University to study mathematics. Ian was a young man of vast promise; this promise, however, was not to be fulfilled. Ian Hope drove his car into the New Forest in 1967, where he committed suicide by carbon monoxide poisoning. Depression had tragically overwhelmed him; he had done less well than expected in his first year exams, he had, apparently, developed personal problems ... in the end he could not cope. His death stunned the school; he had been well liked by staff and fellow students alike.

Terry Trousdale and Keith Pollard were good friends, both in 5W in 1964-5. By a tragic coincidence they both died at 16, both of cancer. Terry had quite a large role in *King Lear*, and it came to light later that his painful illness had already begun when the play was taking place. Courageously, he battled on over several nights of performances, impressing in the part, showing talent that, alas, was soon to be extinguished. Terry died in the February of his fifth year. Keith, having worked hard for his 'O' levels and completed most of them despite his affliction, sadly died before the results came out. Had he been able to hang on to his life a few weeks longer he would have had the satisfaction of knowing they were excellent.

The school's life was, alas, to be affected by much more tragedy.

John Price was a member of 2S in my first year's teaching; I taught him for four years and got to know him very well. On one occasion Terry Goodall, a colleague from geography and P.E., and myself were looking for volunteers to go and help a blind lady in Wales, whose garden had become overrun with weeds. John and two of his friends came happily forward and laboured away zealously for hours. He was unfailingly cheerful, had a tremendous sense of humour and a fine attitude to his studies. He became Head Boy in 1968-9, and was a valuable member of the rowing club where his irrepressible optimism had an extremely positive effect on morale. In the school magazine of 1967, John wrote an article on the thrill of gliding:

> It is a tremendous feeling to know that you are now one of the few people to have experienced this joy. The world is a kaleidoscope of blues and greens, the wind ruffles your hair and the flying wires sing as you bank and turn over the earth 1000 feet below. Alone on the wing you feel great!

Flying became John's passion and he joined the R.A.F. Not long later we heard that he had been killed when his plane blew up during a refuelling exercise.

In 1971, in the absence of Mr Hedges, a special staff meeting was called by Geoff Townsend, the Deputy Head. There had been an accident at the school camp. Keith Briscoe had died. What exactly had happened remains a mystery to this day. One theory is that after the boys had been swimming in a stream nearby, and had then been called to evening meal, Keith had gone back to the stream for some reason, perhaps to collect his spectacles. The boys then noticed his absence from the table and, returning to the stream, found him drowned. He was fourteen, as nice a lad as you could wish to meet, polite, sociable, conscientious. Academically he was almost certainly the number one out of over 130 boys in his year. His promise was enormous. I never taught him myself, but knew him from the table tennis club I was running at the time, of which he was a keen member. Some time later Keith's father came to see me at school and asked if a trophy could be instituted in Keith's name. Rick Stewart from the Silversmithing Department made the trophy, an attractive silver bowl, which was to be awarded to the player of the year. Mr Briscoe bravely came along to the club a few times and presented the trophy to the winner at the end of the year.

Stephanie Dean was a beautiful girl in both appearance and personality. I taught her in her fifth year and she showed great character to battle through from an unfavourable position to gain a grade B in the 'O' level. When she was a sixth former she contracted bone cancer and died at nineteen. I can picture Stephanie now, jumping around the school foyer the day the results came out, full of joy at her successes. When I got home a thank-you card awaited me, signed by Stephanie and her friend Gill Jackson. I treasure it still as a memento of a lovely girl.

John Caveney, Barry Kirkham, John Biles, James Whitfield, Peter Davis, Mike Ellis, Stephen Brand, Tony Collins, David Peskett, Peter Sandbach, Kim Beech, Charlie Mack, Laurence Weaver, Stephen Whittle, Anthony Moore, David Jones, Alison Jones, Claire Smith, David McIntyre and Clifford Nixon were others who met an early death.

Death is difficult enough to accept when it comes to an elderly person who has lived a full and long life; to hear, time after time, of the demise of young people, their future cruelly snatched away from them, is deeply saddening.

The Headmaster Kenneth Hedges had had coronary problems at the age of 47 (in 1967), and had had to take a few months off school as a result; none the less, his death from a heart attack at a Rotary Conference in Blackpool one March Saturday in 1973 shook the school to its core. It was the caretaker who informed me of what had happened when I arrived at school the following Monday morning. An atmosphere of shock and bewilderment prevailed in the staff room. Special assemblies were arranged: Geoff Townsend would take the Senior Assembly in the hall and John Sands the Junior in the gym. I went to the gym. Normally a fluent, confident speaker, John could scarcely get the words out as he paid a moving tribute to the man under whom he had worked for fourteen years.

Kenneth Hedges was a man of quality who had led the school effectively and imaginatively since its inception. He was, too, a man of compassion. His secretary Elsie Whitson told me of two examples of this. She had to go into his study and break the news to him of Ian Hope's suicide, which had a shattering effect. His face turned ashen, he put his head down on his desk and he wept helplessly. Later, when Elsie herself was hospitalised, he went to see her every lunchtime, without fail, until her release. Further, his tireless work with the Rotary Club on behalf of handicapped children (he opened the school every Saturday for them) gained him the great honour of an O.B.E.

Arnold Banford, a pupil in the school in the sixties and later a governor, gave his view of EPGS under Kenneth Hedges:

> Sure, exam results were important and the school performed with credit academically, but they weren't everything. The school helped prepare you for life, and people's strengths were nurtured. Mr Hedges was a man with a social conscience and he was keen that pupils should have one, too. He had a very enlightened view on education and its role in society.

What a pity it was that Mr Hedges did not live to see the completion of a project very dear to him, the construction of a cardiac recovery bed, intended for the Royal Liverpool Children's Hospital. A willing team of sixth formers, under the leadership of Head of Engineering Dick Sears and metalwork expert Paul Haskew, took on the job, overcoming various technical problems and financial constraints en route. The bed was finished by the end of 1973, enhancing the school's already high technical reputation still further. How Mr Hedges would have rejoiced in that, and how glad he would have been that his school had produced something that would help save children's lives.

Kenneth Hedges also had a keen sense of humour. I was once waiting to go into a classroom for the first lesson in the afternoon session when the registration going on inside it seemed to be taking an eternity. Mr Hedges came by, asking what the problem was. I could see that one of our reverends was noting down the religion of the pupils in his form, which was part of the routine administration at the time.

"The reverend's taking down his denominations," I replied.

"The dirty beast!" remarked the Head.

Back in 1959, when, in the temporary absence of a proper staff room and Head's study, the staff and Head shared a classroom divided by a partition, John Sands started to whistle a well-known classical air in the staff section of the room, only to hear the Head take it up and continue to whistle it on the other side of the partition.

In one assembly Mr Hedges was advertising a brass ensemble concert whose ticket prices had been reduced.

*Ellesmere Port Boys Grammar School staff, 1972*

*Back row (L–R): Peter Harrison, Barry Dykes, Brian Nugent, Barrie Shore, Bob Evans, Bob Percival, Steve Yandell, David Scott, Malcolm Deall, Doug Webb, Peter Murphy, Dick Sears, Graham Mercer. 2nd row: Huw John, John Chiverrell, Jeff Jones, Paul Haskew, unknown technician, Marian Latimer, Derek Beck, Gareth Jones, Graham Proctor, Colin Williams, Bill Dean, Mr Coward (technician), Jerry Dawson (technician). 3rd row: Brian Shepherd, John Young, Russ Jackson, John Henderson, John Weir, David Leedham, Ron Durdey, David Prince, Bob Mottram, Nick Ansell, Chris Tune, Malcolm Perry, Ron Lloyd, Edna Evans (technician). Front row: Keith Muscott, Athol Barrington, Jim Summersby, Gordon Linnell, Geoff Townsend, Kenneth Hedges, John Sands, Joan Boggis, Veronica Huntingford, Janice Thompson, Malcolm Pugh, Paul Lewis, Jack Thomas.*

"Get your ticket at the special offer price — no strings attached," he announced.

To me he was always a fair man, and I know that most staff would agree with me on this point. If anyone crossed him badly, however, it could be very difficult to get back on good terms with him.

There seems little doubt that his early death was hastened by the stress he was under at the time. Elsie mentioned Keith Briscoe's comparatively recent death at the school camp in this connection, and Geoff Townsend thinks that an £18,000 claim against the school following an incident in which a boy, finding the gym open but empty, had gone in alone and badly injured himself when falling from the trampoline, was another contributory factor.

However, almost certainly the main cause of the pressure Mr Hedges was under was the worry that he might not, at 53, be appointed Head of the new comprehensive, which was to replace the two grammar schools in 1974.

Whatever the causes may have been, the school had been dealt a blow from which it would not easily recover; the man who had led it from its beginnings to its becoming an established Cheshire grammar school, able to hold its own academically, in the sporting field and in the domain of music and drama, was gone.

## Chapter Nine

With the school due to turn comprehensive in September 1974, some eighteen months after Kenneth Hedges died, Geoff Townsend became acting Head Master for the interim. Geoff had been Deputy Head since the mid-sixties, and he had revealed a notable gift for running meetings; he could always gauge the mood of a gathering accurately and spoke very lucidly. He had also shown himself to be very forward-looking for the time by introducing the Design for Living course to the school, a course later modified into Personal and Social Education (P.S.E.). He was further an excellent assessor of personality and wrote splendid testimonials. Between 1973 and 1974 he seemed to grow in stature and rise to the formidable challenge that confronted him.

He did not, however, become Head of the new comprehensive. Peter Emery, coming to us from a comprehensive school in Partington, was the man selected.

Mr Emery was not quite the commanding figure that Kenneth Hedges had been, but somehow the school ran kindly for him. Personally I felt very favourably disposed towards him and would never have wanted to let him down. I always felt that he dealt with me fairly and on the one occasion that I crossed him, I can see that I earned his wrath. On one very cold morning I had gone over to the Senior Hall in my anorak, and had made a couple of announcements at the start of what was to be Keith Muscott's assembly still wearing it. I learned that Peter Emery regarded this as very slack and unprofessional and I was duly rebuked. A personal black mark, but it was good to know, none the less, that we were dealing with a man who set standards.

As the Head of the new comprehensive, he faced some difficult decisions in trying to bring together the two old grammar schools. One of these was what to do about department heads, since in both schools each department had, of course, had its leader. To avoid unnecessary clashes and bitterness, he appointed joint Heads of Department, and time was to prove him right in his judgement.

He was guilty of the odd amusing faux pas. Once, when announcing sports results in assembly, he declared that so and so had won the javelin in 26 minutes 42 seconds! On another occasion, when a quite enormous lady had been appointed librarian, he announced:

"The school has a new librarian in the shape of Miss ..."

Mr Emery's staff meetings, littered with long and obscure words that sent some staff subsequently scurrying to their dictionaries, could be hard going, like wading through thick mud at times. He was also, along with some of his cohorts, partial to overuse of the latest educational jargon, which led to a certain member of the English Department dubbing them Peter and the Jargonauts.

However, under Mr Emery the new school prospered and became a much pleasanter place than some of us had feared. Further, staff soon knew that on a personal level they had a basically kind boss, concerned, as Head of York House John Young found out during his serious illness, for their welfare. This view would be strongly supported by a female member of staff, who broke down completely when telling Mr Emery about her impending divorce, and received the most sympathetic treatment from him.

Geoff Townsend became one of the Deputy Heads under Mr Emery; Lesley Neill, from the staff of the girls' grammar, was the other. She was a tallish, rather gaunt woman with her hair held back in a bun. No one on the end of a rapid-fire tongue-lashing from her, delivered in a quite superb far-back accent, her eyes seeming to be popping out of her head as she harangued on and on (one member of staff dubbed her 'The Screaming Skull'), would ever dream of answering her back. Even the sixth form held her in considerable awe.

She had a highly individual way of dealing with problems and, being army-trained (she reached the rank of sergeant-major), was never embarrassed by pupils coming out with the odd swear-word. Indeed, her own language could be quite colourful. She once had to deal with a maths class whose teacher did not have the best control and had complained to her that the pupils were always passing wind in his lessons. Lesley came straight to the point when addressing the class:

"Your behaviour is going to improve, and there will be no more farting in this class!"

One boy was brought to her for having urinated into another's shoe on the school field.

"Confess, boy! Did you piss in the shoe?"

No answer, followed by several repetitions of the question, each one showing an increase of irritation.

"Once and for all, DID YOU PISS IN THE SHOE?"

"Yes, miss," avowed the boy, contritely.

"So you pissed in the shoe, then, did you? Well, let me tell you, young man, there'll be no more pissing about! And you certainly won't take the piss out of me!!"

In another incident, a boy had had his trousers removed by three others. When these were duly brought to justice, she lined them up in the school foyer, with the order:

"When I reach the count of three, you will all drop your trousers! Right! One, two, three, drop!"

They obeyed, shamefacedly. No one disobeyed Lesley Neill.

A certain book that was being studied in fifth year English lessons contained passages of an overtly sexual nature, with the result that some parents complained. A meeting was therefore convened to discuss the book; Mr Emery, the Deputy Heads and the joint Heads of English were to be there. Lesley, slightly late for the meeting, breezed in saying:

"All this fuss for nothing! There's nothing in that book I haven't done myself!"

Even Lesley could commit the odd gaffe, however. Peter Murray, looking extremely young when in his first year's teaching, was screamed at by Lesley in the Senior School foyer:

"You, boy, come here! Where's your school tie?"

I heard of one grammar school ma'am in the area who had remarked in her staff room:

"What on earth are we going to do with all these common children?" at the thought of comprehensivisation; in truth I never heard anyone at EPGS talk like that, although I know that those of us who had taught only at the grammar school felt apprehensive at the advent of the comprehensive. Inevitably academic levels could never be the same, and what behavioural problems might arise?

I had had my first taste of 'promotion' in 1967 when Mike Harrison had left and Mr Hedges had given me an increase for taking over Latin. This, in fact, was no longer an onerous job; the number of pupils taking Latin had declined to such an extent that by the time I took over, just a handful of sixth formers were studying it. Then, in 1972, the Head asked me to become a Head of Year, awarding me a further pay rise. This meant that I was pastorally responsible for 134 third year boys, a reasonable number that I thought I could cope with. I was given a fair amount of time in which to do the job, and I was happy with it. I managed to interview every boy during the year, to find out how each one was doing, how he saw his future prospects and what career he favoured.

It was decided that the year group system would be jettisoned in the comprehensive school in favour of a house system. The grammar school had had houses, but in effect they were only really used for sport. Now, though, with five new house names selected, they would take on far greater importance. The names chosen were York, Tudor, Stuart, Hanover and Windsor, after the dynasties of the British monarchy. Each house would contain about 320 pupils, and would have a head and two deputies. Applications were invited for the fifteen posts concerned.

I think one of the reasons I survived in teaching for so long was that I knew my limitations. In truth I would have been quite happy simply teaching and helping with sport, and I was always anxious, unlike Mr Sinatra, not to bite off more than I could chew. The year group job I had found manageable, but there would be a sizeable difference between running a year containing 130-odd grammar school boys, whose ways and likely behaviour I was well acquainted with after what was now ten years' experience, and managing a house of over 300 pupils of all ages and eventually of a great range of academic proficiency. I therefore decided to apply for one of the Deputy Head of House posts, which I duly landed.

I was put in Stuart House, whose Head was chemistry teacher Jessie Land. Dave Prince, who had replaced Dave Brown in the German Department in 1970, was my fellow deputy. Dave had earlier taught in Germany and in what must have been a horrendous school in Liverpool, where the methods of discipline were positively Dickensian. In his first few days there Dave was teaching a class one afternoon when a bell was sounded in the middle of a lesson; he wondered if there was a fire or a fire practice, but the bell was in fact signalling that a flogging was about to take place in the school hall and the whole school was to be there to watch it! In front of several hundred observers, some hapless miscreant was led onto the platform and the Headmaster proceeded to dish out six of the best!

Dave Prince had actually found himself against Dave Brown for the post of Head of German at Bedford Modern School in 1970. Dave Brown was appointed, but was sufficiently impressed by his rival to recommend him to Mr Hedges, who duly contacted him and invited him to apply for the Ellesmere Port job.

I well remember Jessie taking our first Stuart House assembly, and how nervous Dave and I were, wondering how it would go. In fact, of course, there was only one year of comprehensive intake in the hall; the rest, from year two to the upper sixth, were the pupils of the two ex-grammar schools. The assembly passed uneventfully. And later, when Stuart House became fully comprehensive following the departure of the last 'grammar school' sixth form in 1980, there were never problems in the assembly. In the boys' grammar, on the other hand, a few pupils had occasionally become rather less than docile, with the odd strange noises being heard.

There was one memorable assembly at the end of a term in the grammar school when amusement spread unstoppably over the hall. Suddenly, above the strains of "Immortal, invisible, God only wise," an appalling retching sound was heard; a few minutes later, a small boy, his face white as a sheet, was seen being helped from the hall by two members of staff. Then, a few moments later, two further boys, their backs covered in vomit, exited too.

Jessie had been involved in raising money for the Guide Dogs for the Blind in the girls' grammar school, and was keen to continue this. The Guide Dogs, therefore, became the Stuart House charity. We organised an evening's carol singing around the streets near the school, and a good number of Stuart pupils came along. This became an annual event, one to which I always looked forward. Sharing happy times together whilst helping others at the same time — what could be more in the Christmas spirit? These evenings helped to give Stuart House its special identity and to cement pupil-staff relations.

For the most part, however, Jessie, having started out full of enthusiasm, was finding the Stuart House job very stressful. She found that there was a heavy emphasis on the need to discipline; although the number of pupils involved in this was not large, none the less it was they who took up all the time. This, of course, left less time for the pleasanter students, who were in the vast majority. It was this more than anything that frustrated Jessie and really got her down. After two years, therefore, with her health becoming increasingly affected, she resigned from the headship of the house. She had been an excellent colleague to work with and was a very caring person.

Keith Muscott, from the English Department, who had become my co-deputy after Dave Prince was made Head of Modern Languages, was appointed the new Head of Stuart House, as I confidently expected would happen. So confident was I, in fact, that I had opened a book on the event:

No offers Keith Muscott 8–1 Graham Proctor 8–1 Graham Mercer 20–1 bar

I made a nice profit, but it was Barbara Hodkinson who landed me in trouble. After she walked in to be interviewed, she remarked:

"I don't expect I've got much chance. I'm 20–1 on Gordon Linnell's book!"

John Sands discreetly took me to one side over the matter and I was told quite unequivocally not to repeat the exercise.

# Chapter Ten

In 1967 I organised a third year party for the year group which included my own 3L and 3Y; it was to incorporate a variety show. The late John Price, then in 5S, was keen to be in the show; I knew that he and David Herring did an excellent take-off of Peter Cook and Dudley Moore. John Brumby of 3L was to be the stand-up comic, and some of the staff, including Keith Muscott on guitar, got a group together to back me singing *Won't you come home, Bill Bailey?* and *Hand me down my walking cane*.

John and David went down well, John Brumby held his audience excellently and the staff— well, they just about got away with it, and for me seeing my form really enjoying themselves was a great reward for the effort of the organisation.

And so, in 1975, when trying to think of ways in which to raise money for the Guide Dogs, I hit upon the idea of the Stuart House Show. Dave Prince, Robin Rogers and I, with Jessie's full support, left no stone unturned to put together something good for the audience, who, for their part, left no turn unstoned. No, maybe it wasn't quite that bad, but the staff play that we performed in that first show, which one of the English Department had found for us, was utterly pathetic, a supposed comedy that wasn't funny at all. The show was saved by some decent acts from the kids, who came forward in large numbers when the rehearsals began. We made some mistakes in that first show, but we learned from them. We would know what sort of thing to leave out next time and what to leave in. And we would write our own comedy sketch.

Accordingly, Dave Prince and I wrote *It's all the Raj!*, which was set in India at the time the British Empire was still at its height. We did, however, take the anachronistic liberty of referring to an incident in a recent test cricket series in which certain Indians accused the English bowlers of putting vaseline on the ball. There were also references to TV shows popular in the seventies, *Andy Pandy* and *Yogi Bear*.

## IT'S ALL THE RAJ!

*Characters:* Ram Jam Butti, Colonel Carruthers, Colonel Watt, Russian waiter, Indian chief, Irishman, Yogi.

*Prologue* (curtains still closed)

RAM JAM BUTTI: (bowing to audience) Good evening, honourable sahibs and memsahibs! My name is Ram Jam Butti and I'm helping our esteemed British friends Colonel Carruthers and Colonel Watt maintain order here in Poona. You'll meet them in a moment, but first I want to tell you something else— I am the Poet Laureate of Poona, and I'm sure you'll agree that anyone who's Poet Laureate is a Betjeman than you are, Gunga Din! Anyway, I'm going to give you an example of my Ars Poetica right now! Are you ready? Good! Concentrate very hard because it's very, very profound! (pause)

> There was a young man from Darjeeling
> Who went on a bus down in Ealing
> It said on the door
> Don't spit on the floor
> So he carefully spat on the ceiling!

And there's plenty more where that came from! (exit)
(curtains open)

CARRUTHERS: By Jove, it's hot out here, what, Watt?

WATT: Dash it all, Carruthers, it certainly is, what?

(crowd noises off stage)

CARRUTHERS: Gad, Watt, the natives are revolting!

WATT: Oh I don't know, old boy, they're not such bad chaps, really!

CARRUTHERS: No, I mean they're rioting! It's an insurrection!

WATT: (going to window) Must be this dashed heat! You know, last week they caught a rebel by the Ganges!

CARRUTHERS: Dashed painful for the poor blighter!

WATT: Good God, man, they're coming thick as peas!

CARRUTHERS: Only one thing we can do then!

WATT: What's that?

CARRUTHERS: Shell them!

WATT: No, actually, I think it's all right, now ... the chaps have it under control. I think we can relax. By Jingo, it's hot out here!

CARRUTHERS: Dash it all, Watt, it certainly is, what? Well, I suppose we'd better get on with the chores... .

WATT: What chores?

CARRUTHERS: I'll have a vodka, if you don't mind!
WATT: And I'll join you! Need a drink after all this excitement! Waiter!
RUSSIAN WAITER: (entering) Vodka coming up, sir!
WATT: Are you Russian?
RUSSIAN WAITER: No sir, this is my normal speed!
CARRUTHERS: I say, you're new here, aren't you? Where are you from?
RUSSIAN WAITER: Vladivostock, sir!
WATT: I say, watch your language, my good man! And answer the question!
RUSSIAN WAITER: Vladivostock, sir!
CARRUTHERS: Look here, you're asking for a good horsewhipping! Just who are you?
RUSSIAN WAITER: One of the Volga boatmen, sir!
WATT: That's obvious from your language! And which one of the boatmen?
RUSSIAN WAITER: One of the Trotskies, sir!
CARRUTHERS: I thought you were walking funny! Tell me, is it cold where you come from?
RUSSIAN WAITER: It certainly is, sir, especially in the Urals!
WATT: We're lucky, we've had indoor ones put in!
RUSSIAN WAITER: Will that be all, sir?
WATT: Yes, thanks, you may go.
(phone rings)
CARRUTHERS: I'll answer it. Hello, Carruthers here ... Oh, hello, old boy! ... (to Watt) It's the Maharajah of Baroda ... (to Maharajah) Yes ...Yes ... (to Watt) They're inviting us for dinner ... (to Maharajah) Thank you ... next Monday ... splendid! ... capital! ... Thank you, Maharajah ... yes, fine ... rajah and out!
RAM JAM BUTTI: (entering, singing to the tune of the old Pepsodent advert)
You'll wonder what happened to the Indian team,
When you grease the ball with Vaseline!
Did I hear that you are going to the Maharajah's for dinner?
WATT: You did!
RAM JAM BUTTI: A question of the natives trying to curry favour, if you ask me!
CARRUTHERS: No one did! Where the blazes have you been all afternoon?

RAM JAM BUTTI: Watching television, colonel.
WATT: Must have been remarkably interesting!
RAM JAM BUTTI: Yes, sahib, one of the best Indian programmes!
CARRUTHERS: What's it called?
RAM JAM BUTTI: Andy Ghandi, sahib. But actually, my favourite programme is on the radio!
WATT: Which one's that?
RAM JAM BUTTI: Gurkah's Playtime! Sahib, during the adverts on the telly I made up another of my celebrated poems. Do you want to hear it?
CARRUTHERS: Do we have to?
RAM JAM BUTTI: It's very, very good, sahib. Listen!

> There was an old man from Calcutta
> Who got lost down a very large gutter
> He walked right along
> Not minding the pong
> There's no doubt that he was a nutter!

WATT: Actually, Carruthers, old bean, I'm rather looking forward to that meal with the Barodas. His wife makes an excellent curry!
CARRUTHERS: Hot stuff, old boy!
WATT: Yes! And the curry's not bad, either! And she dresses so well, the Maharani ...
CARRUTHERS: Yes, the way most of these Indian women dress, it's a sari state of affairs!
(knock heard)
RAM JAM BUTTI: (Goes to door— returns) It seems there's a yogi to see you, sahib!
WATT: Oh? How did he get here?
RAM JAM BUTTI: In his Lotus, sahib!
CARRUTHERS: Must be something of a poser, what?
WATT: I'll go and see what he wants. (goes to door) Hello, what can I do for you?
YOGI: Hello, Booboo! ... Have you seen my friend Huckleberry Hound, ye, ye, ye?
WATT: No we haven't, sorry! Dashed funny bounder!
CARRUTHERS: I say, Watt, have you heard the latest test score?
(Ram Jam Butti sits and writes)
WATT: The chaps were 305 for 2 at lunch!

CARRUTHERS: Dashed good show! Nice to see them giving the Indians a drubbing, what, Watt?
WATT: Rather! Did you know the whole of our test team has been fed on curry?
CARRUTHERS: So that's what gives them the runs!
WATT: We'll be doing a good job out here if we can teach these people cricket and polo. By the way, Carruthers, do you like polo?
CARRUTHERS: Oh, yes, nice and fresh, just a hint of mint ...
WATT: Not that polo, Carruthers, the game!
CARRUTHERS: Oh, that polo! Oh, rather, old bean! Tophole occupation if you ask me!
(enter Irishman in wellies)
WATT: I say, where do you think you're going?
IRISHMAN: Top of the mornin' to you, sir! I'm just off to the paddy field!
WATT: That reminds me, Carruthers, did you hear about the Irish water polo team?
CARRUTHERS: No!
WATT: All their ponies got drowned! (phone rings) Yes? ... Watt! ... Watt! ... no, that is me name! ... I keep saying Watt because it is my name! ... Right! ... yes ... yes .... Cheerio!
CARRUTHERS: Who was that?
WATT: Ivor E Tusk.
CARRUTHERS: Ivor E Tusk? Oh, you mean the elephant man!
WATT: Yes, it was a trunk call!
RAM JAM BUTTI: It's finished, sahib!
CARRUTHERS: What is?
RAM JAM BUTTI: My very latest flight into poetic fancy!
WATT: Oh, not again!
RAM JAM BUTTI: This is my pièce de résistance!

> There was a young girl from Madras
> Who decided to sit on the grass
> But this was quite damp
> And soon she had cramp
> And shooting pains right up her ...

CARRUTHERS: Ram Jam Butti! There's no need to finish it, thank you very much! You wouldn't want to offend anyone, would you?
(enter Indian Chief)
WATT: Who on earth are you?

INDIAN CHIEF: Me Running Bear. But they can't touch you for it.
CARRUTHERS: But how did you get into this sketch?
INDIAN CHIEF: They tell me it for Indians!
CARRUTHERS: Yes, but not your kind of Indians!
INDIAN CHIEF: They speak with forked tongue! Me stay here!
WATT: But you can't— this is India!
INDIAN CHIEF: Me stay!
CARRUTHERS: Look here, old boy ...
INDIAN CHIEF: Me stay!
WATT: But why do you want to stay? It's not for you!
INDIAN CHIEF: Me stay because me have reservation!
RAM JAM BUTTI, WATT, CARRUTHERS: Kindly leave the stage!!
(exit Indian Chief, muttering)
WATT: By the cringe, it's hot out here!
CARRUTHERS: I say, Watt, do you like Kipling?
WATT: Don't know, old bean, I've never kippled!
CARRUTHERS: No! I mean the other Kipling!
WATT: Oh, him!
CARRUTHERS: Yes, him!
WATT: I'll tell you one thing about him— he does make exceedingly good cakes!
CARRUTHERS: I mean the writer ... the one who writes about tigers.
WATT: I went on a tiger hunt the other day, you know! Came face to face with one of the brutes right in the middle of the jungle!
CARRUTHERS: Did it give you a start?
WATT: I didn't need one, I just ran like hell! By God it was hot that day! 120 in the shade! But I avoided it.
CARRUTHERS: How did you manage that?
WATT: I stayed in the sun! Actually, one of our hunters got mauled ... What was his name?
CARRUTHERS: Oh, you mean Claude Bottom!
WATT: Yes! Dashed perilous pastime, tiger hunting!
CARRUTHERS: Well, Watt, another day nearly done. Another day serving the Empire, eh, what?
WATT: Yes, another day keeping them down!
CARRUTHERS: It's a dashed good job we're doing, what?
WATT: By Jove, yes, Carruthers, a damn good job!
CARRUTHERS: How about a song before we retire?

WATT: Tophole idea! Hey, Ram Jam, sing?
RAM JAM BUTTI: I'm not Ram Jam Singh, I'm Ram Jam Butti!
CARRUTHERS: All together!
SONG (to the tune of *Rule Britannia*)

>Up the Empire, Victoria's our queen
>We're the biggest bunch of twits you've ever seen!
>
>Up the Empire, at cricket we're supreme
>In urgent matters though we're thick as clotted cream!
>
>Up the Empire, in Poona we're so hot
>Which is very likely why we talk such rot!
>
>Drag the flag down, it's been up far too long
>That's the only way to end this dreadful song!

**THE END**

    I have been a show business fan since my boyhood and recall with affection the days of *Ray's a Laugh, Take it from here, Educating Archie, Workers' Playtime* and many more from the pre-television era. The influence of these old radio shows is clearly discernible in the scripts I wrote or helped to write for the Stuart House Show.
    The comic Ted Lune was a regular on *Workers' Playtime*. Ted's speciality was reading aloud a letter he had received from his mum in a gormless type of voice, very slowly. I wrote a Ted Lune-like letter for the show and entrusted it to a second year girl, Becky Powell, to perform. It was not easy for an inexperienced performer to do, since it demanded a lot of nerve; if it was rushed, the desired effect would be lost. Becky, though, took to it like a natural, impressing me greatly at rehearsal. On the night of the show, however, she came panicking to me a few minutes before she was due on stage:
    "I can't go on! I've got enemies out there!"
I managed to calm her and she duly went out to face the audience. She put on a flawless performance, drawing laugh after laugh, and by the time she had reached "I must go now because there is a horrible smell from your

loving mum" (emphasising the lack of punctuation in the letter), she had brought off a personal triumph.

Stuart Crow was another to whom entertaining seemed second nature; he was our stand-up comedian two years in succession at 12 and 13 years old, one of the best we 'discovered'. Personal charm, timing, fluency, with a slightly cheeky look about him, he had the lot. His incongruous opening gambit "Have you met my mother-in-law?" had the audience laughing from the start, and he held them thereafter with great skill.

Even by the 1970s, the old sand-dancing act Wilson, Keppell and Betty were long forgotten. I saw them in *The Desert Song* in Hanley around 1955, but how thirteen year old Alfie Thomas knew of them I'm not sure. Alfie's aim was to lead a troupe of sand-dancers in the style of the old music-hall act. Recruits were found to complete the trio, Alfie and his cohorts set about rehearsing with gusto, and they brought off a great success on the night.

Judith France was a student I had taught for French in my lovely first all-girl class of 1975-6. With terrific dedication and drive, she assembled a sixth form girls' dance team, rehearsed them to perfection, and brought off a tremendous opening to our 1977 show with *Boogie Nights*.

Another fond memory is Carla White and Mandy Jelfs' very professional mime act to Laurel and Hardy's *Trail of the Lonesome Pine* and the same duo's take-off of Windsor Davies and Don Estelle's *Whispering Grass*.

And in 1977, Mark Carter, Phil Welch and Pete Jennings were quite sensational dressed as the Three Degrees with their inspired miming to *When will I see you again?*

I believe that relations between the Stuart House staff and its pupils were improved by the "we're in this together" attitude necessary for the show. I certainly got to know many members of the house far better than I would have done without the show, and, as with the carol singing, we were pulling together for a good cause. The show further enabled the different age groups in the house to integrate more easily.

The Stuart House Show became immensely popular by the later seventies. The hall had 300 seats, and usually they were all filled. One year, about 45 minutes before the show was due to start, the queue outside the main entrance stretched a hundred yards or so down the drive. Mr Emery could scarcely believe that so many people wanted to get into school in an evening.

Now and again in the show, we had sailed fairly close to the wind with our scripts. Ram Jam Butti's poem about the shooting pains is an example of this. One year a young comic had added a risqué joke after the final rehearsal:
"What do you get from the Virgin Islands? Not very much!"

In 1977 the sixth form had put on a quite clever sketch in which a young man wishing to hear a radio programme about how to improve your love life accidentally tunes in to one about car maintenance. Double entendres like "rub the oil well into her points," however, got laughs but escaped criticism.

In 1978, though, things went badly awry. A parent in the audience (a local policeman, in fact) took exception to one or two items and acted drastically. Two third year boys (Andrew Evans and Simon Wilson) had written a song which they themselves, dressed as country bumpkins, performed. Entitled *The Old Pitchfork*, it contained the lines

> "Well I was a-lookin' at a certain planet
> Goin' by the name of Venus
> But I rolled over on the old pitchfork
> Which stabbed me in my ...

We ain't be goin' to tell 'ee where that one went!"

In another sketch (written by the sixth form), a 12 year old boy walks into a bar and converses as follows with the attractive barmaid:
"A pint of bitter, please, love."
"Do you want to get me into trouble?"
"Yes, but I'll have the pint of bitter first!"

Our policeman proved anything but a laughing one. He sent letters of complaint to the Headmaster, to the Chairman of the Governors and to the local press.

That week's *Ellesmere Port Pioneer* had its front page emblazoned with "SCHOOL SHOW SMUTTY, CLAIMS PARENT" and the local *Observer* had a similar headline two days later. A reporter came to interview Keith Muscott (now of course Head of House and just as staunch a supporter of the show as Jessie had been — in fact, he took a leading role in one of our sketches) and myself, to hear our side of the story. Keith saw "nothing wrong with a little healthy vulgarity" and expressed pride in the fact that his house had worked so hard to raise money for Guide Dogs for the Blind. The following week's paper held the headline "HOUSEMASTER

> *Criticism exaggerated says Head*
> # SCHOOL SHOW "SMUTTY" CLAIMS PARENT
>
> A PARENT'S allegations about a "smutty" show staged last week at Whitby Comprehensive School have been investigated by the headmaster, Mr. P. J. Emery.
> He and Mr. K. Muscott, head of Stuart House who presented the show, and Mr. G. Linnell, show co-ordinator, agree that stricter "censorship" may be necessary for similar revues in the future, although they maintain that the parent's criticisms were exaggerated.

Ellesmere Port Observer,
*February 3, 1978*

DEFENDS "SMUTTY" SHOW" which, despite its re-use of the word in the original accusation, at least led to a report in which our defence could be heard. Further, the report contained several letters from parents supporting the show.

The next year, Mr Emery, quite understandably, asked to see the whole script of the show before allowing it to go ahead. He could easily have banned it after what had happened, but proved commendably liberal-minded in the matter. It ran, in fact, till 1984. Pete Jennings, who had left the upper sixth in 1979, wrote a pile of sketches and songs for the 1984 show, which was largely his work. I suppose we just ran out of inspiration after that.

In 1986 I liaised with the Parent Teachers' Association to put on *Une Soirée Française* in the Junior Hall. The PTA handled all the catering side of the evening. There were stalls marked 'Boulangerie', 'Pâtisserie' and 'Charcuterie' from which diners could help themselves, and French staff colleague Steve Yandell cooked a massive 'Mounasou', a French dish of onions and potatoes.

I co-ordinated the entertainment. The sixth form girls, attractively arrayed in berets and French-style tops and skirts, helped with some of the songs. Department colleague Anne Gittins brought along her own folk group and contributed several numbers. Head of Music Mike Williams gave his services as accompanist on the piano. Colleague Kath Amos and I sang *I remember it well* in the style of Hermione Gingold and Maurice

Chevalier; amusingly, the microphone on the table in front of us, having remained erect all through the song, suddenly sank to a limp position at its end.

"Ah yes, I remember it well," quipped Kath.

Registrar Joan Long brought the house down with her effervescent *The night they invented champagne* and Joan and I sang a medley of Cole Porter French-flavoured songs. Finally audience members were encouraged to make fools of themselves in an active version of *Sur le pont d'Avignon*. It was one of those evenings that left me on a high for days.

Our attempted repeat of this success in 1987 came off reasonably well, but we were on somewhat shaky ground in putting on *An Italian Evening* when none of us spoke more than a few words of the language. None the less, we had enormous fun doing it, and personally, paying homage to Dean Martin with a medley of his hits was a particular pleasure.

It was in 1991 that I had the idea of Modern Languages Show, as an attempt to boost our department at a time when Europe was about to open up commercially and languages, it seemed, were about to take on increased importance. I introduced the evening, looking back on my own school languages experiences, making considerable mention of Miss O'Brien and how her style of teaching had influenced me and enabled me to feel enjoyment in speaking a foreign language. From then on it was our pupils showing what they could do. Every teacher had prepared scenes in which the boys and girls conversed in French or German; there were playlets set in cafés, post offices, shops, restaurants, streets, there were phone calls, adverts in the foreign language, French or German songs. The Chairman of the Governors was impressed by the pupils' confidence and fluency, and this, I feel, is the difference between young linguists now and those, say, of the fifties. In those days only the academically more gifted did foreign languages, but often they were taught them like Latin and had no confidence at all when called upon to speak in the foreign tongue. These days the spoken part of the work has a much higher profile, and it was notable that in our show even those from lower sets could perform with conviction.

In 1992 there was a National Festival of Languages at Warwick University and schools were invited to take part in playlets which they had prepared. Our upper sixth showed no hesitation in agreeing to participate. I hit on the notion of using an old Dean Martin Show sketch, which I transposed into French under the title *Le Mari Dévoué*. It was about a husband who obeys all his wife's demands, to climb the world's highest mountain, cross the world's biggest desert, and swim the world's largest ocean only to be told that she wants a divorce because he never takes her anywhere! With Mark Jones and Sarah Daniels hamming it up to the hilt in the leading roles, Whitby upper sixth did us proud, with an award to bring home to show for their efforts. One of those moments when teaching seems the best job in the world!

The school was putting on *Joseph and the Amazing Technicolour Dreamcoat* in 1993 and, to my surprise, Anne Rushforth, from the Music Department, who was the show's producer, asked me to play the part of the French brother. This, in fact, involved doing just one number, *Canaan Days*, but I was more than a little apprehensive about singing on stage with members of the senior girls' choir, of whom, having heard their terrific performances in a long series of concerts, I was somewhat in awe. Anne, however, gave me a backing track, which enabled me to rehearse the song ad infinitum at home. In rehearsal, after an unsure start, I became more and more confident, and on show nights lost all fears and inhibitions, reaching out, going for everything. The feeling was quite indescribable.

# Chapter Eleven

When Mr Emery retired in 1982, Mr Ron Fletcher replaced him as Headmaster. He was a history graduate with a strong sporting background, having played rugby league for St Helens during the sixties and having shown considerable prowess as a boxer in his student days. His large size, together with his stentorian tones and the impression he gave that he would take absolutely no nonsense made him a commanding figure, one that you would cross at your peril. His very candid, direct way of speaking meant that everyone knew exactly where they were with him.

Jack Thomas happened to be in Mr Fletcher's office one day when the phone rang. It was a governor of the school whom the Head regarded as something of a trouble-maker. There was no mistaking the message:

"I hear you go around frightening people. Well, let me tell you you don't frighten me!"

He also had a nice line in gentle sarcasm. One day, when he noticed one of his Heads of Department proceeding through the foyer wearing a rather loud pair of trousers, he remarked with a smile:

"Good morning, Mr ... , going on holiday, I see!"

Former Deputy Head Geoff Townsend said of him:

"He was excellent at spotting the potential ability of people and a good developer of their strengths."

The gruffness in his manner could appear intimidating at times, but underneath it beat a good heart and you were aware that you were dealing with a man who tried to be fair to everyone. Further, staff knew that if any undisciplined student or any unjust parent was causing them problems, they would have their Head's full support. He called in one parent because his son had been guilty of covering a toilet wall with graffiti. After explaining the boy's transgression in full to his father, Mr Fletcher announced:

"I'm afraid you owe us £250. That was what we had to pay for the cleaning job."

There was no objection. The parent turned angrily to his son, telling him:

"You are going to pay for this. I'm going to sell your music centre and your computer games!"

And the school got its £250.

If the school was in any way threatened by external forces, we were happy in the knowledge that Mr Fletcher, like the John Wayne or Gary Cooper characters in the movies he so admired, would come out with all guns blazing to protect it. As far as developments in education were concerned, Ron Fletcher stayed, to continue the analogy, always one step ahead of the posse, his ear close to the ground, seeming to know what was about to happen before it actually did.

Around him he gathered a strong team as the eighties progressed.

Fiona German-Lloyd, eventually given the title Director of Studies, became one of the key figures in the running of the school. Fiona is the kind of devotee every school needs, giving of herself unstintingly to its cause, working all the hours God sends, caring passionately about the school's welfare. Collaborating with the Head on the timetable, a task at which she was brilliant, able to see the ramifications of a move well ahead of its being effected, organising the curriculum, liaising with the PTA as its secretary, in addition to coping with a good size teaching commitment and running the archery club, Fiona went about everything with maximum conscientiousness and minimum fuss.

Gareth Jones was one of the Deputy Heads; a good organiser, expert money-raiser, efficient, executing all his tasks with extreme promptness, always calm under pressure. Gareth's subject was biology; he once had an amusing confrontation with a parent. Gareth, facing the assignment of introducing the facts of life to a year seven class, spoke of abortion and caesarean operations, but told the pupils that what they learn in class should at this stage be secondary to what their parents tell them at home; if there was anything further they wanted to know, they should tactfully ask their mother and/or father. The next day Gareth had an irate parent on his trail at school. The parent's son, over the previous evening's meal, had bluntly remarked to his mother and father:

"Mr Jones said I had to ask you how often you had sexual intercourse."

Gareth explained that that was not quite what he had said, which the parent eventually accepted.

"Oh, incidentally," said the father by way of a complete non sequitur as he was departing, "can you tell me why it is that my urine goes red when I eat beetroot?"

Another of Mr Fletcher's deputies was Penny Temple, a German teacher of flair, style and boundless verve who enjoyed good relations with pupils, preferring for the most part to disarm rather than threaten. Penny was well up with educational trends, always very well read concerning the latest developments. She was also a very caring person. There was one particularly unenviable task she took on herself. The husband of a maths teacher, Caroline Marron, was killed in a car crash; it was Penny who went round to see Caroline, to console and sympathise, to do everything she could to help a colleague whose world had just fallen apart.

Penny was also an ardent flyer of the flag for English grammar, ultra-keen that pupils and staff alike should have a good command of the workings of their native tongue. And rightly so!

John Sands, my former Head of Department, was a third deputy. John was now in charge of the Junior School (years 1–3, later named 7–9), dealing with pastoral and discipline problems with all the old industry and thoroughness he had brought to the running of our department. John developed an effective technique in dealing with doubtful characters hanging around the school entrance or encroaching onto the grounds. He would run towards the intruders with his camera, snapping them at regular intervals on the way. They invariably took fright and flight.

After John's retirement in 1988, Russell 'Two Sheds' Jackson was appointed Deputy Head. Russ had first come to the school in 1970, then later served a three-year teaching stint in Oman. Now he found himself, among other things, in charge of the school budget, a key job these days when a school manages its own financial affairs, and which demands long hours of labour. Russ took to it willingly, and, as a later inspectors' report was to confirm, ran it very efficiently. For all the pressure he was under, however, Russ never lost his sense of humour, as was evidenced one day in his workshop.

When a certain male member of the Art Department began coming to school in an ear-ring, Russ and Jeff Jones (also from Crafts) decided to imitate. Having slipped pieces of brass wire into their earlobes, they set off in pursuit of their colleague down a corridor, walking like hippies, snapping their fingers. When they got to the staff room, one rather naïve colleague remarked:

"Hey, you fellows are wearing ear-rings! How did you get them on?"

"Well," said Russ with conviction, "Jeff held my ear in one of the vices, then punctured a hole in it with a needle. Then I did the same for him."

"Gosh!" said their gullible friend, "It must have hurt!"

In the late eighties Ken Oliver became master in charge of the Junior School. Like John Sands before him Ken soon realised that it was a job which often showed you the worst side of the children: you were spending a lot of time dealing with pupils sent to you by staff for causing trouble. It could, therefore, be quite wearisome at times, but Ken, for all his conscientiousness, never let it get him down too much; in fact, if there was one person guaranteed to have a new (mostly!) joke for you in the staff room, it was Ken. He helped keep my morale up on many an occasion. When Ken was a boy, he used to run home from school every lunchtime to hear *Workers' Playtime*. He and I often amused each other with brief games of "Whose catchphrase was this?" when we passed on the corridor.

In 1989, Dave Prince, the Head of Modern Languages, left the school. Dave had given fourteen years of his life to an arduous job during which time the department had had to adapt to various changes. In 1975 the school was one seventh comprehensive; by 1989 the full transformation, with all its attendant pressures on staff, had long since taken place. Exams also changed a good deal during that time. The old 'O' level and CSE disappeared, the GCSE came into being with its heavier weighting on listening and speaking and consequent increased demand on the Head of Department in the organisation of oral exams. Dave had also been heavily involved in the Reutlingen exchange for the whole of his time at the school, giving up a large percentage of the 'recovery' time of his holidays to do so. He had been a very successful Head of Department, but the mighty efforts that he had made plus their accompanying stresses had taken their toll. Dave went into insurance for a year, then took a teaching post at Abbey Gate, a private school near Chester, where he saw out the final years of his career. There, he rejoiced in the fact that all he had to do was teach; the minimum of admin, much less in the way of meetings — which can be extremely wearing after a day's teaching, and which, regrettably, seemed to increase in number as the years went by at Whitby. At Abbey Gate, free of all the extra stresses, Dave could dedicate himself to the education and entertainment of his pupils, at which he was an expert.

Dave departed, Mr Fletcher now had the idea of forming a triumvirate to run our department, with Steve Yandell as Head of French, Chris Tune Head of German and myself as co-ordinator. I had to give up the Deputy Headship of Stuart House to do this, and had some regrets about this, but after some fourteen years of doing this job, perhaps a change might prove beneficial.

Steve had taught in the school since 1968 and was now well-established after, like myself, a not altogether convincing start. As Head of French he was a very unselfish man, often electing to take poorer classes himself when he could have passed them on. He had his own highly idiosyncratic style of doing things, and always seemed laid back; in fact he put an enormous number of hours into his work.

His staff room jokes could be somewhat obscure, leaving listeners wondering whether they themselves were less intellectually gifted than they had supposed or whether Steve's *plaisanteries* were simply so esoteric as to be beyond normal comprehension. On one occasion Steve declared to a recently arrived and totally mystified French assistant that he was "mother of pearled". I myself had no idea what he was talking about, let alone someone whose grasp of English was far from secure. Steve then proceeded to explain that the French for 'mother of pearl' was 'nacre', and he was in fact knackered!

I had learned about the language arpo from Mike Hughes, a German teacher who had a brief sojourn at EPGS in the sixties before deciding that teaching was not for him:

"I just can't take seriously saying to a boy 'What, boy, you've lost your book? Monstrous!' "

Arpo had been used to fool the Germans in the war, apparently. To speak arpo, all you had to do was to put 'arp' into every syllable you spoke; for example, 'good' would become 'garpood' in arpo. Steve and I would often converse in it in the staff room, something along these lines:

"Garpood marpornarping, Starpeve! Harpow arpare yarpou?"

"Varperarpy warpell, tharpank yarpou! Arpand yarpou?"

"Farpine! Arpi harpear tharpat yarpou arpare narpow arpa Darpean Marpotarpin farpan!"

"Parpiss arpoff!" concluded Steve, who, as I well knew, much preferred Frank Zappa to Dino.

If someone really caused Steve irritation, he would simply exclaim dismissively "Linctus!", which, as everyone should know, is for coughs.

Chris Tune, who had also arrived in 1968, was similarly intrigued with words and was regularly making puns. For example, after I had told Chris that the following year's French trip would be to Rouen, he asked me:

"Will you be calling at Raques on the way?"— going to Raques (rack) and Rouen (ruin) (!). This was the sort of thing flying about the room all the time the three of us were together.

"Why is my mate breeding sea-birds?" I asked one lunchtime. Shaking of heads. "Because he believes one good tern deserves another." Groans all round.

"Why is my mate giving all his friends trilbies this Christmas? Because he likes to make his presents felt."

"Linctus," said Steve.

Once Chris had come into the staff room following a conversation in the corridor with a certain lady teacher who tended to get very close to you when addressing you, thrusting her not inconsiderable bosom into whatever part of your body (according to your height) was opposite it. Chris announced:

"I've just had a tit-à-tit with ..."

Chris was very hard-working, and could usually be seen making his way to his car at the end of the day weighed down with enormous piles of books for his evening marking session. He was a very good team member, ever helpful to his colleagues, and a quality teacher.

Something that happens now and again with the less bright sets in the comprehensive set-up that never used to happen at all in the grammar school is the sudden non sequitur placed in the path of your lesson quite ingenuously by one of the class. Once Chris was taking a lower third year set, speaking to them in the target language, when all at once a girl on one side of the room chirped up to one on the other:

"What bra size are you, Cathy?"

Ron Durdey was once describing the Spanish Armada to a second year class, and was pleased to see a girl's hand go up, thinking, naturally enough, that his lesson had captured the girl's interest.

"What football team do you support, sir?" she asked. Ron, taken somewhat aback and having no interest in soccer, replied hesitantly:

"Well, I don't suppose I support any, really."

"What? A big strong boy like you!" exclaimed the girl.

Ron was one of the staff who taught in the grammar and the comprehensive. The idea that a pupil could have spoken to Ron in that semi-cheeky way would have stupefied the grammar school boys he had tutored; they were in awe of him and showed him every respect.

One of the first tasks awaiting the triumvirate was a meeting with the governing body to discuss the department's policy. Penny Temple, also present, told us afterward that we had acquitted ourselves very well. This was also the time around which the Modern Languages Show had taken place, which gave us further good publicity.

But in fact almost from the start I was not happy in this post; the side of the job which has to determine departmental policy, then work out the implementation of the policy document, then decide our policy on equal opportunities, then on differentiation, et cetera, et cetera interests me little. All this, which in John Sands' day would have been left to common sense, now took time and energy which I preferred to spend or expend on more meaningful tasks.

There was also a certain vagueness about the job, and if I was not sure, for example, whether Steve or I should be doing something I usually left it to Steve, who, having been Head of French since John Sands became Deputy Head, had had experience of it.

After a while the Head and Penny realised the system wasn't working, and I was switched to a new role, curriculum development in languages. Penny and Mr Fletcher had for some time harboured the notion of a language awareness course and one of my new briefs was to devise and develop it. This really caught my imagination; it was something tangible, something certain to be worthwhile, something I could really get my teeth into. I got down to work immediately, borrowing and buying books galore, getting ideas from these, putting in other ideas of my own, and drawing up a first draft of the course.

The Language Awareness Project was to be done in year seven over a three week period half way through the year, during English and modern languages lessons.

For years teachers in the school had been complaining about the poor grammatical knowledge of pupils, even those well up the school; I therefore devised quite a large grammar section which would be incorporated into the English part of the course, giving full coverage of nouns, verbs, adjectives, adverbs and so on. There were further features on place names and their origins, old English, middle English, pidgin English, the origins of words, the runic alphabet and local words.

For the Languages Department section of the project I compiled a cassette of samples from several languages. Apart from the French and German assistants I used different members of staff who had knowledge of other languages; Penny knew Swedish, Shauna Holloway Spanish, Mike Cleaver Italian, Russ Jackson spoke both Arabic and Welsh, Roy Dale Russian and two pupils, Joyce Yung and Abdul Aziz, one of Chinese origin and one of Indian, recorded Cantonese and Hindi respectively. The 'taster' in each language consisted of "Hello," "How are you?", "Very well, thank you," "Goodbye" and the numbers one to ten.

Other features were to be studying words from different languages that had strong similarities to each other — 'Country Cousins'; a look at Latin, how it had invaded the English language and how it was still used in churches, in certain phrases ('post mortem', for example) and in mottoes — Everton and Tranmere F.C.s were two good local instances; a study of different alphabets — Chinese, Russian and the origins of the letters of our own alphabet; a look at how words from all over the world had come into English, with special features on Italian and French; studying a world map of languages and working out which were the most commonly spoken ones.

Once I had written the whole course in longhand, it had to be computerised. I was still a novice in this field, but Nikki Perry, fairly new to our department, was an enormous help. Covers were designed for the books, and thanks to Nikki and Brenda in Resources, the whole thing looked quite professional.

I think the course was a success; certainly Penny and Mr Fletcher were happy with it, and, as far as I heard, it went down well in lessons.

Another task set me was devising a Business French course for the sixth form, mainly intended for those who wanted to carry on with the language, but who were not taking 'A' level. The course was to be a practical one for those who might one day work in France or for a firm in Britain that needed someone with a working knowledge of commercial French. This, too, proved stimulating work and I had it ready for September 1992. It turned out that fewer people were able to take it than had originally enrolled (due to timetable constraints), but those who did were keen and interested and for me the lessons were always something to look forward to.

Mr Fletcher had also asked me to arrange work experience abroad for these FLAW (Foreign Languages at Work) students, and I was able to liaise with Madame Mahdi (our current French assistant's mother) for them to work in shops in Villeneuve-sur-Lot. They were all eager to go, and when they returned the increase in their confidence was clearly discernible and their affection for France and the French considerable.

A further part of my new duties was to introduce other languages into the sixth form curriculum. I decided to start with Russian; we had a fluent speaker on the staff in Roy Dale who was very keen to teach it. We elected to use the St Martin's College, Lancaster course and what turned out to be a faithful band of students was recruited.

It seemed logical that the 'A' level students should be given the opportunity of doing work experience in France as well as the Business French people. Accordingly, in November 1995, John Peet, Head of Modern Languages at the nearby Catholic High School, and myself went over to Toulouse on a pioneer visit for which Pauline Sidwell, Senior Languages Advisor for Cheshire, had paved the way via an acquaintance. John and I visited two Lycées Professionnels (Business Schools), sampled excellent hospitality from the staff, and the spadework was completed.

In 1996, with Debbie Tacon as accompagnatrice, the first Cheshire schools work experience visit to Toulouse took place. John Peet swore that the experience was worth an extra grade on their 'A' level result, and I certainly would not want to disagree. Again, increased confidence and fluency were noted upon the students' return, and they had every right to feel proud of what they had achieved. It does take some courage to offer your services to work, say, in a French primary school or a shop or a hotel; you must know that there will be uneasy moments when you don't understand something, when you just have to smile your way through. And courage, too, to accept to stay with a French family for a fortnight, a family you know little about, on whose sympathy and kindness you are entirely reliant. Thus far, though, the Toulouse-Cheshire exchange has worked well.

Mr Fletcher also asked me to take over the running of Sponsored Day. Organising this means that you are, to all intents and purposes, in charge of the whole school for that day. The aim of the day is simply to raise as much money as possible for school funds; by the late 90s this reached around £3,000 a time. Pupils gained points for indoor (eg computer games, darts, ping pong) or outdoor activities (eg shots at goal, tennis points, basketball nets) and for correct answers to a 50-question quiz; their sponsors paid up according to their points total.

For part of the day pupils watched feature films in the main halls. My job was to co-ordinate the whole event, which meant staffing all the activities, devising the quizzes, and choosing and booking the films.

A few years ago there was a likeable lad in Stuart House called Tripney, whose parents (no doubt Virgil fans) had lumbered him with the christian name Aeneas. One Sponsored Day a boy in his form, in answer to the quiz question "What are cumulus and nimbus?" had written "Aeneas Tripney's middle names."

Sports Day was always one of my favourite days on the calendar. Watching athletic prowess was to me always gratifying, especially that of pupils who were not so gifted academically. It was during the eighties that the P.E. Department asked me if I would like to do the announcements over the P.A. system on Sports Day. I was delighted to do this, and decided to risk an innovation — to give a commentary on each race. I did not, of course, know the name of every athlete participating, but at least I could identify their houses from the colours they were wearing. These commentaries became a kind of homage to Peter O' Sullevan, filled with typical O'Sullevanisms like "as they race towards the line," "turning into the straight with a commanding advantage" or "coming there strongly on this side," and tended to give Sports Day something of a racecourse atmosphere. So much so, in fact, that one colleague asked me if we were installing a tote next year!

# Chapter Twelve

The school cottage is situated in the countryside near Dolwyddelan in North Wales. Opposite it towers the daunting-looking Moel Siabod, whose ascent was always a feature of a cottage weekend. I went several times there, including a 1967 visit with my own form, when John Wolfenden and David Leedham were with us. The telling of ghost stories as the boys huddled round the coal fire on a chilly night or walked through the nearby forest at a late hour was a regular feature of those weekends.

At that time the cottage was a damp, cold place; a newspaper placed under a sleeping bag at night was soaked by the following morning. In your twenties, though, I suppose you'll put up with anything! There was always a strong feeling of comradeship; everyone had to pull his weight to make the weekend work. It was arduous, though; getting through Monday's teaching was never easy after a weekend at the cottage.

The cottage had a Racasan toilet, which needed emptying on the Sunday afternoon before departure. If anyone had transgressed badly during the weekend, he would be the one to empty the toilet into the nearby pit. One particular visit, Steve Yandell and I were with a third year group, one of whom was the likeable but slothful 'Slug' Collins, whose sins had been of omission rather than commission, and the burden of emptying the toilet became his. We told him to be careful, since it had been raining and the grass along which he had to carry the toilet was slippery. Poor Slug! He lost his balance completely and the toilet fell on top of him, leaving him totally covered in excrement and urine! How the other lads laughed, myself too, until it dawned on me that Slug was due to travel back in my car!

I had been deeply impressed by Paris during my own trips there (my first to France, in fact) in 1962 and 1963. The first time I visited the city part of me seemed to stay there, and even now a lot of the enchantment remains. Therefore, in 1964 I was only too keen to accept Dave Taggart's invitation to officiate on the first year trip there. Dave, who was number two to John Sands in our department, had given me some useful tips during my first year. He was a good teacher in the traditional mould, who knew how to entertain a class at the same time. Sometimes great laughter could be heard coming from his room, but Dave was always fully in control. None the less, he was prone to the odd bout of temper, as miscreants found to their cost. One day a class expecting one of the reverends as its normal teacher planted a wonky chair at the front of the room behind the teacher's table. Their horror when Dave entered, explaining that he was replacing the absent reverend, can easily be imagined. He promptly sat on the set-up chair, which immediately collapsed, with Dave being sent crashing to the ground. A thunderous outburst of rage ensued; none present would ever forget the incident.

Seeing the famous monuments again, but this time, as it were, through the eyes of the twelve year olds I was with, who had never seen them before, brought all their initial impact and a strong sense of wonder back to me.

One day we were due to visit the Piscine Deligny, a swimming pool built actually on the River Seine. I calculated that we could walk to it from our base at the Lycée Molière in the Avenue Victor Hugo, but it proved to be further than I thought and the weather was oppressively hot. After

*The school cottage, with Moel Siabod in the distance.*

about an hour, colleague Gwen Dunn, mercifully out of earshot of the children, demanded:

"How much bloody further is it? I'm buggered as Barney's bull."

In 1968 and 1969 I took part as a courier in the Crewe-Mâcon exchange with my friend Wesley Dixon. This was organised by Crewe Town Council, since Crewe and Mâcon were twinned towns, both having a railway industry. The Crewe children spent three weeks in Mâcon, then the French youngsters a similar length of time in Crewe. It was very demanding on staff involved and took up the whole of the summer holiday; I am glad now, though, that I stuck it out, because I learned a good deal of French in Mâcon.

Wesley had done a year as an assistant in France, actually in Mâcon, and he was clearly more knowledgeable than I was. I recall his ability to conduct a meaningful conversation with a Frenchman about the latter's gravel path, which would have been beyond me. In reality I learned from Wes just as much as from the French themselves, so perfect was his command of the language. He would organise a couriers' visit to every house where an English child was staying, and these sometimes went on for hours. My French came on by leaps and bounds.

One night we were invited out for a special meal on the occasion of the 21st birthday of the female courier in the party. We sat down at the table at 8pm, and, several courses, several drinks, several conversations and several songs later arose from it at 3am, still to this day the longest session I ever spent at a dining table.

As couriers we were not paid, but we had our accommodation (in a boarding school vacant for the summer) and our meals free. Wes thought the meals in the "Rocher de Cancale" were excellent, but sometimes I was less impressed; indeed, it might well have been having to try to eat some of the items on the menu in Mâcon that sowed the seeds, as it were, for my later conversion to vegetarianism. Pigs' trotters, for example, appalled me, and I could only manage one mouthful of andouillette (a skin bag filled with chopped intestines) before wanting to vomit. One night, as we were leaving the restaurant, a van arrived and a man proceeded to carry a large trayful of frogs' legs into the kitchen for the next day's meals. Since the frogs had only recently been killed, however, the legs were still moving merrily around on the tray!

I partnered John Wolfenden on a second year EPGS trip to Paris in 1970. We stayed at Vitry, a few miles from the city centre but handily placed for the metro. The conditions in the Comité d' Accueil centre at Vitry were among the most spartan I experienced in all the trips I went on. There were 28 of us, 2 staff and 26 boys, in a dormitory that wouldn't have been comfortable for half that number.

One morning John awoke with a boy's hand and arm right across his face! The toilet facilities amounted to one repulsively malodorous hole in the ground between 28 people. One evening, after a visit to a fairground, there was a queue of some sixteen to use it; disastrously, an unfortunate boy who was about eleventh in the line did his business in his trousers before he could make it to the hole! A new pair of underpants from the Monoprix on the Champs Elysées became one of our priorities for the next day!

Neil Rathmell, from the English Department but very much a Francophile, and myself ran a trip to Chinon in the Loire Valley in 1971, which went well with lots of laughs, and I was under the impression that the boys' behaviour had been 100 per cent good. Later on, however, I was told that young Pilling had sneaked out of the dormitory in the middle of the night, had borrowed a boat moored by the side of the river and had proceeded to row downstream for some considerable distance before eventually rowing back and returning to the centre. And there were Neil and I, sleeping through the night, content in the thought that all the lads were safe in bed!

In 1972, on the Rouen trip that Steve Yandell and I led, there was an evening when we allowed the youngsters to have a glass of wine with their meal, which many French parents do. One lad, not exactly God's gift to the French language or to social graces, asked me how to ask the lady serving us for more wine. I told him to say:

"Encore du vin, s'il vous plaît, madame."

A few moments later, as the waitress passed his table, thrusting his glass under her chin, he demanded:

"Vin!"

Coming back to the hotel one evening when the boys had been allowed out with the proviso that at no time were they to be alone, Steve and I were convinced that walking ahead of us down the street were two of our lads, smoking. We crept up stealthily behind them, and were about to pounce when one of them turned round — a puzzled-looking young Rouennais! An uneasy "bonsoir", then back, giggling stupidly, to the hotel.

The hotel where we stayed in 1974 at Paramé, near St Malo in Brittany, had a balcony (onto which all the upper rooms led) that was so unsafe that the building was closed down after our visit. The somewhat grumpy proprietor was dubbed 'Bruno' by the kids, after the dog in the Longman's Audio-Visual French Course. I had one or two pleasant conversations with him — he just seemed to hate young people! He told me as we stood on the rickety balcony looking down on his cabbages that he and his wife had collected 75 pink snails from the vegetables the previous Sunday and had eaten the lot as the first course of their dinner.

Two events marred our 1976 trip to La Panne in Belgium: the coach driver's very unhealthy interest in our fifth year girls and a case of theft.

It happened twice on our trips that coach drivers, who are with us for the whole of our time abroad, took a fancy to some of our girls, and on the second occasion these were only fourteen years of age! This, needless to say, is the kind of stressful situation you can well do without when you already have the responsibility for the safety of a large number of young people. On both occasions strong words needed to be said before the visit could continue as planned, but both trips finished peaceably.

A boy was caught shop-lifting in a souvenir shop in La Panne. I had taken some of the group to the cinema, while the other teachers were on duty around the beach area. I was called out of the cinema and went hastily to the shop where the owner was threatening to call the police. In the end she backed down, but even now I find it difficult to forgive this boy; he had the reputation of being a tearaway in school (though not a thief) and it was only by a narrow verdict in his favour that I had allowed him to come to Belgium. This was how he repaid me! Looking back I can see that I should not have taken him; at the time I thought he could repair his damaged reputation by doing well on the trip. These days things are much tighter; every pupil wishing to participate has to have the signed approval of his or her house staff. This works well. In recent years there have been few problems, and certainly no near- brushes with the law!

By the 1980s Anne Gittins had joined the French Department. She was an excellent teacher who, although she would stand no nonsense from her pupils, none the less loved them dearly. She would often address them as "my beautiful children," which not too many teachers could get away with. But there was no unease when Anne referred to them in this manner; they knew that she really did love them and expected them to be good in return. Anne is a living example of 'amor vincit omnia'.

Anne was with me on the 1982 upper sixth trip to Paris, when I saw quite the most remarkable piece of street entertainment I've ever witnessed. We were at the top of the glass-enclosed escalator situated on the outside of the Pompidou Centre when we noticed, way below us in the courtyard in front of the building, that a crowd was gathering, apparently around two figures we could just make out. As the escalator descended we could see that these were two men, who, despite the cold of this February morning, wore only trousers. Eventually the escalator reached the ground and we joined the crowd, which by now had grown quite large. One of the men stood shivering, covered from his neck to his feet in chains and padlocks. The other made his way around the throng, collecting money. As he passed where we were standing, I noticed several things about him; he had a medal pinned to his naked chest and his back seemed covered in small holes. There were two further holes in his lower cheeks, just to the sides of his mouth. On the ground nearby was a large sack, bulging with objects that at this stage were a mystery. At length he judged that he had sufficient money and announced:

"Le spectacle va commencer!"

He went over to the sack and took from it an ordinary light-bulb and a hammer. Placing the bulb on his upturned palm, he smashed it to pieces, then proceeded to consume all the broken glass of the bulb! Returning to the sack, he withdrew a wooden 'bed' covered in nails that looked at least nine inches long. He lay back onto the bed, and the man in chains stuck his foot into his colleague's chest, forcing him right down into the nails. He made no sound, however, as he lay.

I was still wondering about the holes in his face, but the mystery was soon to be solved. Two long, thin steel needles were the next items out of the sack. The first he forced into his left cheek, then through his mouth and out of his face via the right cheek. The second needle was forced through the skin in front of his Adam's apple! Then he announced:

"Et maintenant mon collègue va se libérer en trente secondes!" whereupon the second entertainer, by dint of a whole series of wriggles and contorsions, managed to rid himself of all the chains and padlocks before the appointed thirty seconds had ticked away!

The 1987 trip to South Brittany was the first on which we took a video camera. After our return, ever-helpful Dot Lloyd from Resources patiently showed me how to edit the film and add a commentary and some incidental music. So, complete with microphone and some Poulenc played by Rubinstein on cassette, I recorded a French commentary to go with the

17 minutes of film I retained from the original. We had years of use from it and lots of amusement, too, as the pupils and staff grew older and thus more open to gentle mocking when seen on screen.

Anne had the idea on this trip of blowing a whistle during the evening meal, this being the signal that, until a second blast was heard, everyone must speak only French. The idea worked well once the children had got used to it. Its effect on teachers' digestive systems wasn't too favourable, however; we had to leap from our seats and move around the tables interviewing the children.

During the sixties and seventies a trip to France was simply that. We always encouraged the pupils to speak as much French as they could in the shops and cafés and so on, but they were not given specific tasks to carry out. It was Anne who changed that, introducing worksheets so that the visit had a working side to it. Everyone had to:

1. Converse with a teacher about what they had done on that particular day
2. Count out French money in front of a teacher
3. Identify shops in the street
4. Find out information from an Office du Tourisme
5. Fill in their own identity card in French
6. Send a postcard to a teacher back home
7. Keep an account of what they had eaten and drunk
8. Note supermarket prices

This gave an extra sense of purpose to the trip, and I think it pleased most parents to think that their children's education was continuing while they were enjoying a holiday.

Another feature of the 1987 trip was a visit to a French secondary school at Crozon in West Brittany. Anne knew one of the staff there and arranged the visit. Our pupils got to meet French children and interviewed them as part of their project. We dined there, too, discovering that French school meals have an extra touch of class compared to the English equivalent.

Brittany or Normandy had become our usual holiday destination by the end of the eighties. The lovely beaches, picturesque and historically interesting towns and the local customs that are worth investigating — we had, for example, a terrific evening of Breton dancing in St Brieuc — together with their comparative proximity to England, make them ideal for a school visit.

In 1992 there were five staff on the trip, Mike Cleaver, Nikki Perry, Debbie Tacon, Steve Yandell and myself, and the usual number (forty-odd) of children. At first things ran according to plan; coach from school, arriving in Plymouth with time to spare, then leaving for Roscoff on the Brittany Ferries ship *Quiberon* on schedule, weather set fair. We were just over half-way through the journey, less than three hours from Roscoff. I had made my way up to the top deck when I heard, coming from somewhere below, a detonation. People looked at each other in alarm. Soon black billows of smoke were invading the deck, and seven horn-blasts were sounded, the signal for passengers to gather at the life-boat stations. Within a very short time the deck was filled with concerned-looking people, parents and children in search of each other, pupils and teachers likewise. We got our group together as best we could among the milling hordes, hastily but trying not to cause a panic, with Nikki, Steve and myself counting one part of it on one side of the deck, whilst Debbie and Mike had the rest of them assembled some yards away. Mercifully the count revealed none missing.

Then crew members, grim-visaged, began distributing life-jackets. Clearly we were going to abandon ship. Nikki looked at me with considerable apprehension, we instinctively hugged each other. I looked at the life-boats around the deck as the crew began to prepare them for descent into the sea. Surely there weren't enough for the thousand-odd travellers we could see around us? Meanwhile we supervised the giving out of the life-jackets to the children, finally taking and putting on our own. Then, a desperate cry from one of our girls:

"I haven't got a life-jacket!"

Nikki, right by her and at that moment some yards from Steve and myself, immediately gave her hers; anxious moments passed before she was able to acquire another and don it quickly. Some of our girls were blubbering unashamedly; boys and girls alike had looks of utter bewilderment on their faces. I cannot pretend that I was not inwardly frightened by this sequence of events; I thought of my lady friend back in Nantwich and wondered if I would ever see her again. If there had been one explosion on the ship, could there not be another at any moment? It was a brief reflection; there were forty children to think about.

Gradually the story of what had happened filtered through from the crew. There had been an explosion and a fire in the engine room. The fire, they said, was under control. There was no need for panic. The engines had been stopped. It occurred to me that the fire might not be under control at all, that we were being told this to prevent panic; certainly the crew still looked very stern-faced. These thoughts, however, I kept to myself, and tried to spread reassurance among the worried young faces around me.

Three Royal Navy Sea King helicopters arrived, wheeling round in the sky above us until one of them descended to a point just above the *Quiberon*, and an officer was winched onto the deck. We found out later that the captain had sent out a mayday message which had been intercepted by Land's End Radio, who had contacted the Royal Navy. Other ships came on the scene, their presence to a degree comforting. The threat of abandoning ship, however, was still a real and dreaded one.

The order to climb into the life-boats, though, still did not come. Passengers began to sit down on the deck in the very warm sunshine; the crew appeared carrying refreshments for everyone. Things began to seem calmer.

Debbie meanwhile had tuned her transistor to Radio Four for the news bulletin and was hit by the full force of the tragedy. An engineer had perished of asphyxiation by fumes whilst trying to put out the fire in the engine room. This awful fact would explain the expression on the crew's faces. The blaze was, however, now extinguished.

So the fire was out. But surely the engine room would still be as hot as hell? Surely the captain would not risk restarting the engines? Did he still plan to abandon the *Quiberon*?

Back in Ellesmere Port the rest of the staff, the pupils having broken up for the summer holidays, were involved in a teacher training day. During their coffee break, however, some of them caught the BBC 1 news, the first item of which, to their immense horror, was the *Quiberon's* accident. Penny Temple began phoning relatives of pupils and staff on the trip, telling them not to panic, the boat was drifting. Debbie's daughter Joanna, then just ten, received a garbled version of Penny's message from their Japanese child-minder, whose English was not good. Joanna was dreadfully distressed until, on a later news bulletin, she could make out her mother, clearly alive and well, on the deck of the ship.

The hours went by with nothing, apparently, happening. The sun beat down relentlessly to the discomfort of many, who had nowhere to go to get out of it. Some of our party became badly blistered.

Eventually two tugboats arrived. The captain had finally made his decision; the *Quiberon* would be towed to Roscoff. The boats took up their positions, one to the starboard side of the prow, one to the portside, and the long, slow operation began. Progress was not easy; the ship rolled about a good deal despite the very moderate speed. Many passengers started to vomit over the side. The new danger, that of capsizing, was certainly not imaginary; Steve, never one to panic easily, expressed his considerable apprehension, but only to his colleagues.

The journey went painfully on and on and darkness fell. What should have been a six-hour passage was now, provided it was completed safely, going to be at least three times that long. No lights could be switched on. Torches had to be borrowed from crew members for toilet visits. The toilets themselves could not be flushed and stank to high heaven. One part of the deck was covered in urine which had overflowed from the latrines.

It was well after midnight when we finally limped into Roscoff harbour. Cheers of relief resounded as the stricken vessel completed its somewhat ignominious voyage. Our party was told that since it was now too late for us to carry on into France by coach, we must come back onto the ship after it had been cleaned up to spend the rest of the night in the cabins. As we disembarked TV crews, radio and press reporters descended on us. I gave two interviews, one for French television and one for a Breton newspaper, in both of which I recall saying:

"L'équipage a été magnifique."

The crew certainly had been magnificent in a freak situation, helping passengers all they could for hour after hour, showing extreme kindness and patience despite the loss of one of their number. They had also, it later transpired, worked like Trojans to prevent the fire from spreading.

Going back on board the ship was really the last thing we wanted, yet we had no choice. None the less, having the cabin doors rapped upon very early the next morning when we were still trying to sleep off the effects of our ordeal seemed the last straw!

A year later I was conversing with a fifth form boy about his holidays during the recording of his GCSE speaking test. This boy had been on the 1992 trip. I have often wondered how taken aback the examiner marking the tape must have been when hearing me ask the boy:

"Tu avais peur au moment de l' explosion dans le bateau?"

The rest of that holiday passed without further mishap, but what had happened on the *Quiberon* did, inevitably, rather cast its shadow and many children became anxious when they were due to board the return

> **Un groupe de collégiens anglais :
> « L'équipage a été magnifique »**
>
> « On a appris qu'il y avait un mort sur le bateau en écoutant la radio anglaise au bulletin d'information de 15 h ». 3 h 30 samedi matin. Les 40 jeunes collégiens d'Ellesmere Port près de Liverpool viennent de débarquer du « Quiberon ». Dans le hall du passage en douanes où les formalités sont exclues, les jeunes anglais sont regroupés en compagnie de leurs accompagnateurs. Gordon Linnel, l'un des cinq enseignants qui encadrent les adolescents, reprend le fil de la journée, les traits tirés par la fatigue. Comme l'ensemble des 1.124 passagers du car-ferry, les collégiens ont gagné le pont à 12 h 30. « Soudain, il y a eu beaucoup de fumée. Nous avons rassemblé les enfants et nous sommes dirigés sur le pont supérieur ». Distribution des gilets de sauvetage. Préparation des canots... « Graduellement, la fumée a diminué. Aux premiers instants, certains enfants pleuraient. Mais dans le groupe, il n'y a pas eu trop de panique. La présence des hélicoptères, des avions et des autres bateaux était rassurante », souligne l'enseignant à l'image de tous les commentaires saisis au vol lors du débarquement.
> Et de répéter : « l'équipage a été magnifique. Le personnel s'est montré exemplaire ». Les collégiens tombaient de sommeil. Ils ont reporté leur départ pour Granville, leur lieu de destination. Le groupe est retourné dormir dans le bateau. Samedi, il devait prendre la route après le déjeuner lors duquel était prévue « une minute de silence en la mémoire du mécanicien décédé ». Mardi soir, les jeunes anglais et leurs professeurs reprendront le ferry pour l'Angleterre, au départ de Cherbourg.

Le Télégramme,
July 20, 1992

boat. The coach driver was helpful, though, telling them over the coach microphone that he had crossed the Channel eleven hundred times and only this once had anything gone wrong. The ship we sailed home on was a reassuringly enormous vessel; the voyage was accomplished with no further trauma.

One unusual thing happened to me on that trip. We were based in Granville, and one day I was walking through the streets carrying my brief-case which contained documents to do with the trip. Suddenly a man rushed out from a shop, calling to me:

"C'est par ici, monsieur!"

I followed him, wondering what on earth could be going on. When I got into the shop, he indicated a distressed-looking man slumped on a chair in the corner, saying to me:

"Voici le monsieur qui a souffert la crise cardiaque!"

I had to explain quickly that I was not a doctor!

Letting their child go on a French holiday with the school can involve a considerable sacrifice for some parents. Yet if the youngster concerned has the right attitude (and it has been my experience that a large number do), then the benefits, over and above the acquisition of social skills which being part of a group will bring, can be very great. France can become for that young person a special place, one to return to again and again in later years; the French language suddenly becomes something real and practical, indeed indispensable — to speak to an actual French person in France still gives me a buzz even after thirty-odd visits to the country. The wonders of French cuisine can be discovered (it is not all frogs' legs, pigs' trotters or cows' intestines) and French ways and customs can be observed at first hand or participated in. There are many new horizons to be explored. If the young person is sufficiently adventurous, then for the parent the trip will prove a good investment.

## Chapter Thirteen

Most of the subjects that year seven pupils (first formers) will have on their timetable they will have had some contact with before; as far as French or German is concerned, however, they may well be having their first experience of it at secondary school. Of those who have had a taste of a foreign language at primary school, some may have been well taught, but it seems to me, and it is a viewpoint backed up by an OFSTED inspector I was recently in conversation with, that a fair number of primary teachers called upon to take foreign language lessons may lack expertise to a greater or lesser degree. I was once sent to a primary school in Ellesmere Port to watch a French lesson. It was a depressing experience. The lady concerned was speaking English about 95 per cent of the time. The lesson went something like this:

"Now, as you can see, I've got a ruler in my hand. Now who can tell me the French for a ruler?"

Child, in poor accent: "Une règle."

"That's right, une règle. (in equally poor accent — so that's where the child got it from!) Now, what's this? I'm holding a pen, now. What's the French for a pen?"

That first lesson in the secondary school is therefore of vital importance. If the child has no previous experience of the language, then the teacher has the novelty value of the subject in his or her favour and should aim to take full advantage; if the child has been well taught in the language at primary school and has enjoyed it, it is crucial that the first lesson makes sufficient impact to indicate that that enjoyment will be continued; if the child has been subjected to lessons like the one recounted above, then it is essential that the first lesson makes such a strong impression that the bad work that has been done before is smashed to smithereens.

My strong advice to any language teacher would be to hit them with the foreign language from the outset. Do not spend the first lesson talking to them in English about French or France; you can find time for this much later after you have created a 'French' atmosphere as the norm by almost total use of the target language. Lesson one was always for me an hour (or 40 minutes in the grammar school) of all-out effort to immerse the class in simple French. It would go something like this.

At the command of "Entrez!", they stream in, and take their places (standing) quietly — a gentle "Silence" should be enough to give anyone fussing-about the message. When they all look ready you say brightly "Bonjour, la classe!", in reply to which you may well get puzzled looks, smiles or whatever. They may be hearing the phrase for the first time. So you point to yourself, say "Bonjour, la classe!" again, then point to them and say "Bonjour, monsieur (madame/ mademoiselle)!" This will give some of them the message (though probably not everyone). Then say "Bonjour, la classe!" a third time and put your hand to your ear — chances are you will get a fair number of them saying "Bonjour, monsieur!" back to you. "Pardon?" you ask. "Bonjour, monsieur!" — and this time hopefully most of them will have the reply. Then, to consolidate, you dash out of the room, close the door, then immediately re-enter theatrically, declaim "Bonjour, la classe!" and all should now, with fervour, call back "Bonjour, monsieur!"

First fence jumped. Then, moving your hands downwards to indicate a request for them to be seated, give the order "Asseyez-vous!" Most should sit immediately, but a few stragglers may not — a second "Asseyez-vous!" may be needed, with further hand movements. Then, as soon as the last one is seated, a dramatic "Levez-vous!" can be introduced, with hands moving upwards this time, whereupon the majority will stand up again. Repeat if necessary until all are standing again. I found that most children enjoyed this active start, and it was always a pleasure to see smiles on most faces.

My next step would be to tour the class, pointing to girl pupils and indicating "une fille", "une fille", "une fille" and so on, then move to a boys' area, demonstrating "un garçon", "un garçon", "un garçon". Then suddenly "Asseyez-vous, les filles!" You will always find that at least one boy will sit down with the girls. Be careful here! Humiliation of pupils should never be part of a teacher's armoury, but a gentle "Oh là là! Tu es une fille?" should help the boy realise his error. From this, enormous amusement can then be had: "Asseyez-vous, les garçons!", "Levez-vous, les garcons!", "Levez-vous, les filles!", "Asseyez-vous, la classe!" and so on, until everyone understands the commands and can obey them.

Next, a few classroom objects. Again, a lively approach needed. Moving swiftly round the room, tap on an object, name it in French, get class to repeat. Cover "la porte", "la table", "la chaise", "la lampe", "la fenêtre", for example. Practise strongly for 5 minutes, then test them. Point to an object and look expectant. Keep testing until they have a good knowledge of the words. Only on one occasion did this misfire. A boy started to cry during my rapid race around the room. He asked if he could go to the school nurse. I let him, wondering if he might be ill. Later, however, the nurse told me that it was the lesson that had upset him! Still in tears, he had explained to her:

"The man was banging on the window."

By now (say 15 minutes into the lesson), the class, or most of them, should know how to greet someone in French, they should understand two commands and the French for 'girl' and 'boy', and should recognise the names of and be able to name a few classroom items.

Next aim — pupils to be able to name themselves in French. Pointing to, say, a boy and asking "Tu t'appelles comment?" will probably be greeted by a puzzled look. No English, remember! The best way out of this may be to say:

"Possibilité — Je m'appelle Jack. Possibilité — Je m'appelle Kevin. Possibilité — Je m'appelle Stephen."

Hopefully the pupil or someone else in the room will answer "Je m'appelle ..." + his or her name. Then the idea should spread like wildfire around the room. Try to get them to pronounce 'appelle' in a good French accent, not like the ending of the English word 'bell', but bouncing the tongue on the roof of the mouth in a genuine Gallic manner! Most will enjoy the attempt. The shier ones may feel stupid to begin with speaking in a foreign tongue and may need their confidence building up. Be patient with them!

I always feel that it shows the teacher's respect for and interest in his or her pupils if he or she can learn their names quickly, a respect which will be all the more easily reciprocated. In my final year I had a class in which there were Kayley, Kayleigh, Carly, Kylie and Carla, which was quite a challenge. I found that looking at a list of their names again later in the day, having taught them earlier, would help to get to know them more quickly.

Next, go to the board and write the figures 1, 2, 3, 4, 5. Pronounce them yourself, then get the class to do likewise — un, deux, trois, quatre, cinq, several times over. You will usually find that some of them have met the early numbers before, so you should not have a problem finding a 'volontaire' to count aloud from one to five. This too should spread quickly, and within four or five minutes, half the class will have shown they have mastered it; the rest should soon follow. Then on to 6, 7, 8, 9, 10, using the identical method. A few minutes later most will have the satisfaction of being able to count from 1 to 10 in a foreign language. When they have mastered something, be quick to praise: "Bravo", "Excellent" or thumbs up sign or simulated applause gesture. Kids love success. Give it them as soon and as often as you can.

By now, after some 35 or 40 minutes of all-out effort, you may feel like a rest. Fat chance. This is the first lesson and its impact is paramount. Drive yourself to the limit — it will be worth it later!

A sudden "Levez-vous!" and they are all on their feet, hopefully eager for what's next on your bill of fare. You sing *Frère Jacques* for them; they may know the tune already. Then get them to speak the lyrics clearly after you, miming what the words mean or drawing on the board to explain. Then sing it together. Then divide the class into two, one section to the right of you, one to the left. Sing it with the left group. Sing it with the right group. Then do it as a round. Then let any volunteer duos or trios sing it, then any individuals.

We're now inside the final 15 minutes. Time to act out a scene in a French café. Have a Coca Cola bottle handy. Then act out the whole scene yourself, playing the parts of both the waitress/waiter and the tourist in the café.

*Part of my Year Eleven class, 1995, in the room which was my own for the final few years of my career. L–R: Adam Barlow, Lynne Doran, Simon Clark, Claire Edwards, Carl Hayward, Chris Myatt, John Heaney, Richard Wilkinson (almost hidden), Michael Tomlinson, Andrew Dilworth, Mark Rogerson, Stuart Doyle.*

TOURIST: Monsieur! (Madame, Mademoiselle)
SERVER: Oui, monsieur? (etc)
TOURIST: Un Coca Cola, s'il vous plaît.
SERVER: Oui, monsieur … (brings drink) … voilà!
TOURIST: Merci. (drinks coke) … L'addition, s'il vous plaît.
SERVER: Oui, monsieur … (gets bill, puts it on table) … voilà!
TOURIST: Merci. (pays) … Au revoir.
SERVER: Merci. Au revoir.

    The dialogue must be repeated by the class over and over, until it sinks in. Then you play the waiter and a confident pupil can take the tourist's part. This usually works well and gives them the sense that they can now do something in France when they go there. After a while, as the dialogue sinks into more and more brains, they can try this in pairs, which they usually enjoy.
    The final five minutes now. Time for a further run around the room to consolidate classroom objects, then to the board to point to the numbers

and confirm those. Then two or three "Tu t'appelles comment?" and the bell is due.

"Levez-vous. Au revoir, la classe!" Wave your hand. "Répétez — Au revoir, monsieur!"

And off they go. Hopefully they liked their first taste of secondary school French. Maybe one or two didn't; it's hard to please everyone. Chances are, though, that the majority will respond to the energetic approach and perhaps they really appreciate the effort you've put in. Who knows, maybe they'll never forget their first experience of a foreign language. You may be left feeling exhausted, but good seeds will have been sown. If there's another class waiting outside, better summon up your resources all over again!Two other pieces of advice, aimed at newer teachers.

Make the classroom you inherit as pleasant a place to be in as you can. Have attractive material on the walls — maps, posters, pupils' best efforts, and individualise your room with your own trademarks all over the place. And if you have the good fortune to have new or newish tables, the moment any kind of a mark appears, get rid of it. Thus most pupils will grow to respect your room.

Secondly, try to have everything ready for the pupils' entry: all the materials you need should be near to hand. It does not impress pupils to see you faffing around looking for the right transparency or your picture of a packet of frozen peas!

## Chapter Fourteen

The following is a collection of true tales, all but two of them from EPGS/Whitby Comprehensive (later Whitby High), which might amuse.

In the sixties there lived in Whitby village a middle-aged lady called Miss Cumpsey. She was, alas, of rather less than sound mind, and could often be seen walking along the streets near the school looking as if she had no idea where she was.

One summer day, Ron Durdey was conducting a lesson on Bismark's foreign policy on the ground floor; the atmosphere was serious, the pupils were writing away busily. Suddenly, the door opened and in walked Miss Cumpsey, in a diaphanous dress revealing her total absence of underwear. She curtsied respectfully to Ron, then presented an enormous bouquet of weeds to him and exited politely, leaving Ron absolutely speechless. The class, after a few moments of incredulous silence, exploded; the ambiance of concentrated work was utterly destroyed.

Head of Resources Dot Lloyd was one day crossing the foyer when an unknown gentleman came through the front door. She asked him if she could help him and he said he wished to speak to a certain pupil. Dot duly traced the child and brought him to the gentleman. She then hung around just in case the man was not bona fide, but was highly amused to hear him demand of the boy:
"Just tell me where you've put your grandad's false teeth!"

There was a time earlier in the comprehensive era when the bottom set third year did a very general French course which included doing a project on Paris written in English. One girl in my set wrote:
"One evening we went to *Carmen* at the Paris Opera and we all sang along."
How she coped with "Près des remparts de Séville chez mon ami Lillas Pastia" or "L'amour est un oiseau rebelle" was some way beyond my comprehension.

A domestic science teacher, Mrs Jones, late for a staff meeting, finally dashed through the door after the Head had begun the first item on the agenda.
"I'm sorry I'm late, Headmaster," she announced, "I've had some buns in the oven."

When in the sixties a boy from my form came to confess to me that he had been playing truant, he said:
"I'm sorry, sir, I've let the form down. I've been bonking."
Thirty years later, that would have meant something rather different. In Ultima Travel's 1976 holiday brochure, it was stated quite innocently:
"La Panne is full of gay cafés."

Again a case of time changing the meaning of a word; then, the brochure simply meant that the cafés concerned were bright and lively.

In the early seventies the salacious sense of the word 'screw' was just beginning to catch on; in her science lessons, however, Jessie Land had no idea of this and proceeded blithely to address her class as follows:

"Carbon is used in pencil lead. The molecular structure of carbon makes it slide, so it can be used as a lubricant. If you've ever watched your father screwing something, if you rub it with a pencil it will go in much more easily."

Sniggers, especially among the male members of the group, made her wonder what was wrong. When she was later told of the word's new meaning by a male colleague, she was mortified. Even now, all these years later, Jessie says she blushes at the thought of what she said.

When a minibus arrived at school one day for a sports fixture, a team of King's School boys, bedecked in their blazers of broad green and blue stripes, descended from it. A Whitby boy, waiting to play in the game, never having seen the uniform before, remarked:

"God! They've come in their pyjamas!"

Mr Hedges, a keen ballet fan himself, once persuaded members of the Royal Ballet to come and perform in the school hall. The visit was successful and very pleasing to the Head, but he probably never knew of two incidents that arose from it.

During the dinner hour, one of the male dancers was making his way down a corridor when one of our less cultured fourth years shouted after him:

"Hey you, you're a puffter!"

The dancer, fit and muscular from his training, whipped round, grabbed the boy, pinned him to the wall, spat a few choice words at him and left him a quivering, embarrassed wreck slouching against the wall. The offender clearly wouldn't offend again in a hurry.

At that time there was a boy called Duckworth in the school, and it so happened that he was about to exit the school via the main front door at the same moment as one of the ballet dancers. One of Duckworth's friends, arriving in the foyer and wanting to catch his attention, shouted "Hey, Duckie!", whereupon the ballet dancer turned round, furious with indignation until he realised he was not the one being addressed.

The ability to maintain a sense of fun despite all the stresses and strains the job can entail is undoubtedly a desirable quality in a teacher. Andrew Searson, a recently arrived music master, was put to the test by his own form, a year twelve class. Being now sixth formers, they rather objected to having to be in their form room by exactly 8.45 am like the rest of the school, considering that at their age they should have the right to a few minutes' grace in the mornings. Andrew disagreed, wanting, especially at this early stage of his career, to play things very much by the book.

One morning he went into his stockroom to collect his coffee mug, only to discover it was missing. Turning to his form, he asked:

"My mug! Has anyone seen my mug?"

Smiles all round. Andrew realised that something was afoot, that the mug was in fact their prisoner. Then the spokesperson stood up:

"Give us five minutes extra or THE MUG GETS IT!"

Andrew did not let himself down. No display of irritation, no temper. He laughed along with them, and they liked him all the more for it.

A short time later, Andrew's patience was tested further when an envelope appeared on his desk one morning. On opening it he found two items inside: a photo of the mug and a ransom note. But still he managed to smile.

Shortly after this, however, the saga of the mug took on a new twist. By chance Andrew came across his mug's hiding place when looking for something quite different. He did not, of course, tell his form. Now was the time for *his* little joke! Pretending to lose his temper, he ranted:

"This has gone too far! I'm sure the Deputy Head will take a dim view of this! I want my mug back now, or there will be very serious consequences!"

Naturally the class sensed their little game had come to an end. One of them went to get the mug, only to find, of course, that the hiding place was bare. Andrew let them suffer for a while, then revealed the missing object, safe in his possession! And so the episode ended appropriately — with laughs all round!

Stephen Homer was a personable but rather precocious lad I taught for most of his time at Whitby, including his first year. I introduced our attractive French assistante, Florence, to the class and in the first part of the lesson invited them to ask her a question in French. These began to flow:

"Quel âge avez-vous?"
"Avez-vous des frères ou des soeurs?"
"Où habitez-vous en France?"
And so on. When Stephen's hand went up and he was given the all-clear, he asked with a twinkle in his eye:
"On va au cinéma vendredi soir?"
Another assistant, Lamine, came from Tunisia. Once he was talking with a group of lads from my class, telling them how he had to get up at four every morning and walk across the desert to get to school. One lad asked:
"What if you've got a paper round?"

An advisor friend told me of his visit to the classroom of a rather naïve older lady teacher in a school in Lancashire. He noticed that the wall was covered with drawings of huge penises. When she saw that he was looking at these, she remarked:
"Yes, strange, isn't it? I really don't know why they've drawn space ships all over my wall!"

James Leyland, who took his GCSEs in 1995, was likeable and humorous, but definitely a touch lazy. When he was in year eight he amused me with his ironical reply to my question about pop music:
"Quel est ton groupe favori?"
"Mon groupe favori est Foster et Allen."
One week during year eleven he had handed in for homework a letter in French which had been copied from his talented friend Stuart Doyle. It didn't take me long to realise I was reading something I'd already read, but in any case James gave the show away by signing the letter:
"Sincerèment vôtre, Stuart Doyle."

Just before we broke up for Christmas one year, one colleague still hadn't received any Christmas cards from the children. In the lunch hour he was told that a boy was asking to see him in the foyer. There, a first former was waiting for him and held out a white envelope. My colleague took the envelope, and, feeling a card inside it, said to the boy:
"Thank you very much. It's the first one I've had this Christmas!"
When he opened it, his eyes fell upon a dental appointment card.
A hapless member of the Music Department began a lesson thus:

"We're going to start today by singing a song entitled 'My Grandfather's Cock', which stopped, short, never to go again when the old man died.

One wet day, John Sands was teaching French to a not particularly gifted set and was waiting for what seemed an eternity for a boy to answer a question. In his ennui, John inscribed LULU (a comic book character of the time) with his finger in the condensation on the window. Little did he realise what he had started. A few days later LULU was to be found written all over the place, in the toilets, down the corridors, on desks, with the result that the Headmaster announced in assembly:
"I don't know who this girl Lulu is, but the inscribing of her name all over the school must cease immediately."
John was standing near the front. His eye caught that of a boy from his class of a few days before. Knowing half-smiles were exchanged.

Funny, sometimes, how youngsters can pick up phrases from other people in their family and come out with them later in not quite the right way. First former Reggie was given some weekend German homework by Chris Tune. When, the following Monday morning, he failed to produce it, Chris asked him what the problem was.
"I haven't had a minute's peace," he replied.

Brian Nugent was a Head of Year in the grammar school and Head of Hanover House in the comprehensive. His forte was his ability to give a succinct, well-judged résumé of the character of anyone in his charge that you might ask him about. His obsession, however, was the production of mounds and mounds of printed paper sheets. To the tune of "Football Crazy", I wrote this lyric:

### ODE TO B.N.

Oh he's admin crazy, he's admin mad
Administration's taken away
The little bit of sense he had
He's always duplicating
There's nothing he will shirk
Brian'll soon be buried
Underneath his paperwork.

Ron Durdey was once fussily pulled up by a Deputy Head for using the wrong colour when noting something in his register.

"We've got to get it right, Ron," he was told, "it's important!"

Ron, normally placid but on this occasion riled, had a grim retort for his critic, recalling his service in World War II:

"I'll tell you what's important. You're lying on your stomach behind a five-pounder anti-tank gun and a German tiger tank is approaching with the gun trained towards you. That's important!"

Most unusual Christmas present to a member of staff— seriously balding Chemistry master Mike Douglas receiving a pack from one of his classes marked 'Head-polishing Set', containing a can of Pledge, cleaning dust and a yellow duster!

A former Chairman of the Governors, a good-hearted man but not a very well-educated one, was introducing the school choir during speech day. The choir were due to sing *Adam lay y bounden*. The Chairman, however, foreseeing difficulties in the pronunciation of this, said:

"I'm now going to hand you over to the school choir. I'm not quite sure how to pronounce their song, but when I was a lad and I couldn't pronounce a word, my grandma used to say "Pronounce it Manchester." The choir will now sing 'Manchester'."

This same gentleman, at a Christmas social to which teachers and governors were invited, announced:

"Yes, I always enjoy having intercourse with the staff at Christmas."

The number of witty teachers' nicknames in the grammar school was, inevitably I suppose, rather larger than in the comprehensive. Overheard in the sixth form annexe was this conversation between two students, one of whom had what he considered to be a notably boring teacher the following lesson:

"Who've you got next?"

"Morpheus."

I once taught a very sturdily built first former called Derek Mustard. He wasn't brilliant at French, but at least he usually tried to participate in class. One lesson, however, one very warm afternoon, he was slumping over his desk.

"Derek, tu es fatigué?" I asked him. His indignant reaction let me know that he thought I was accusing him of being overweight and of unorthodox sexual leaning.

During the annual school Christmas concert in St Mary's Church, Nantwich, the Head Boy of the grammar school was called upon to read one of the lessons. He began well enough but caused a good deal of amusement to ripple through the pews when he read that the three wise men brought Jesus "gold, frankenstein and myrrh."

When in her mid-fifties Barbara Hodkinson had to take a class of fourth years for sex education. Finding herself faced with a barrage of very personal questions, she retained all her composure.
"Do you still have intercourse, miss?"
"Of course I do! It makes for a much more exciting middle age!"

What happened to physics specialist John Henderson one day was not in itself particularly funny. John always used a starting pistol to enable his pupils to work out the speed of sound, and was checking the gun out, thinking it was empty of shells, when suddenly, as he pressed the trigger, a loud detonation sounded and John was hit above the eye by the exhaust and wadding coming out of the pistol at high velocity. He still bears the marks of the accident. As so often happens in schools, completely erroneous versions of what happened were rife. One boy asked him:
"Is it true that you tried to shoot yourself, sir?"
After 33 years' service, John retired in 1997. He was determined to make a clean break from the school, and when asked if he would be prepared to come back to do occasional supply work, he remarked that that was twentieth on his list of post-retirement plans.
"Twentieth? What's nineteenth, then?" he was asked.
"Death," he replied.

A rather naïve female teacher was amusingly let down by her defective command of the English language whilst taking a sixth form assembly. She was recounting how, on a holiday in Scotland, her car broke down. She was standing there wondering what to do when some workmen gathered round.
"It all worked out all right, though," she went on, "because the workmen all made suggestive remarks to me."
The imagination boggles.

Peter Murphy, complaining of the insensitivity, nay stupidity, of the editors, once showed me a poem from a book of verse ostensibly aimed at third year pupils. The poem, about a highwayman, was called *Dick Straightup*.

Mr Bridge, a portly gentleman known as 'Bubble', was caretaker in the grammar school. At one time he was building a boat, and the Technical Department came up with an alliterative suitable name for it: 'Cheshire County Council's Corpulent Caretaker's Canal Cabin Cruiser'.

The boys caused him untold annoyance (his sense of humour seeming to have permanently departed from him) by whistling the Laurel and Hardy theme every time he passed in the corridor. And if he entered the hall while the school orchestra were tuning up ready for rehearsals, some of them would start up the same tune, to his intense irritation.

It was in the hall one day that Bubble came close to death. When John Sands climbed up into the gantry to switch on the electricity system for the radio to be used in his classroom, he had no idea that Bubble was repairing a fault up there at that very moment. When John pressed the switch, an almighty shock traversed his fat friend, who roared:

"Are you trying to f***ing kill me?"

One Deputy Head was making his way down the corridors of the Science Department about five minutes after the end of break. He came upon a class without a teacher who were kicking up something of a racket. Dashing into the science prep room, he demanded officiously:

"Who's supposed to be taking this class?"

Doug Webb, the Head of Chemistry, strolled over to the timetable on the wall and, having checked what he probably knew anyway, announced:

"You are!"

Jane Gratton had a boy in one of her geography classes whose persistent talking was a regular pain. One day the boy somehow contrived to get his six inch ruler stuck sideways in his mouth. With his eyes popping out of his head, the boy gestured desperately with his pointing fingers for Jane to come and remove it. Rather enjoying the break from his usual nattering, however, Jane told him:

"If you think that I'm going to get that out of there, you've got another think coming!"

The end of the lesson was quite soon enough.

Sometimes pupils can succeed in embarrassing teachers by throwing out the odd innuendo or suggestive remark in a lesson; sometimes, however, this can bounce back on them. John Sands was teaching a fifth form when the word 'putain' cropped up in the passage of French being dealt with. John explained that the word meant 'prostitute'.

A boy called Blair, seeing what he thought was his chance, announced: "Sorry, sir, I don't understand. What's a prostitute?"

If Blair thought he could cause his teacher embarrassment, however, he couldn't have been more wrong. John, looking his questioner right in the eye, explained:

"Oh, you know, Blair, one of those women who sells her body to any man who will pay for her services."

It was Blair, much to the amusement of his classmates, who was made to cringe.

Peter Harrison taught English at the school for 18 years. He was normally the most mild-mannered of men, rarely allowing events in the classroom to rile him. A notoriously bad form, 2E, however, drove him too far one day with their undisciplined behaviour.

"Silence!" roared Peter, at the same time hammering the side of his outstretched hand onto a desk. To the astonishment of the class, the desk lid split right down the middle and fell in two pieces to the floor. The nickname 'Chopper', which was to stay with Peter for the rest of his career, was born.

In the seventies there was a member of staff at the school who, although his attendance for most of the year was good, always seemed to be away during Wimbledon fortnight. I wondered if he was suffering from Gerulaitis. Suspicions that he might be swinging the lead were confirmed when the Headmaster Mr Emery, no less, switched on his TV set and saw his 'ailing' member of staff sitting happily among the centre court crowd!

This same member of staff and myself were in school at about five o'clock one evening when we decided to undertake a very childish prank. Donning some particularly hideous masks I happened to have in school, we ran around the building, appearing suddenly at classroom windows, evoking screams of terror from unsuspecting cleaners and incurring the wrath of the humourless caretaker, who dismissed us as being "worse than the bloody kids!"

Those who consider that male teachers remain essentially boys for ever would no doubt have thought that this episode gave fuel enough to their contention.

Jack Thomas turned a corner into a corridor to find a girl laying verbally into a boy, calling him a "silly bugger!" Jack duly remonstrated with the girl, saying this was not lady-like and asking her what her mother would think.
"Me mum?" replied the girl, "she calls me dad that all the time!"

Paul Haskew had no idea who the man was who willingly helped him to remove the shutters from the windows of the school pavilion for the game against Eaton Hall and then to set up the wickets.
Then a little girl ran up to them and said to the visitor in her thick Merseyside accent:
"Hallo. My name's Karen. What's yours?"
"My name's Gerald," he replied in a friendly tone. The future Duke of Westminster, no less, showing a nice common touch.

One lunchtime Dave Prince, Mike Williams and myself had got into a conversation about bizarre demises. Mike recalled how the French composer Chausson had died when riding his bicycle full tilt into a brick wall. I recounted an incident I had read about in which a man, having completed his business on the toilet, pulled the chain hanging above him before he stood up, only to be mortally injured when the tank to which it was attached fell on his head.
"Well, it only goes to show," said Dave, "you can't beat the cistern!"

During one interminable staff meeting when a discussion on whether girls should be permitted to wear signet rings was dragging on and on, I slipped a piece of paper to long-standing colleague Colin Williams on which I had written:
"Do you think that girls should be allowed to swan around wearing signet rings?"
His reply came back a minute later:
"Only when they are mute."

# Magic Moment

She looks pensive,
Slightly puzzled,
Risks her answer —
The right one!
And suddenly,
Her eyes light up,
Her smile beams forth.
I return her smile
And into the memory store
Passes a moment of warmth,
There to be recalled,
To bring cheer
When in old age I look back
On the delights
Of being a teacher.

       G.L.

# Chapter Fifteen

Half way through the summer holidays of 1993, I was convinced I would never teach again.

The problem had begun the previous December. I had bought a CD of Rachmaninov's choral composition *Vespers*, listened to it on my headset and was very satisfied that the recording was every bit as good as the reviewers had indicated. Some two weeks later, I played it a second time. Something was wrong; on the high notes the sopranos were distorting badly. I played other discs with the same alarming result — high female voices or flutes or French horns, high notes on the piano or anything at all that was played a touch loud, I could not hear properly. Around the same time, a persistent hissing sound started in my right ear. My GP prescribed Stemitil, then Stugeron, but neither had any effect. Homeopathic medicines did nothing, either. The noise, which, I learned, had a name — tinnitus — now spread to my left ear. An appointment with a specialist was made for me for early August.

I was told bluntly that I had lost some hearing, that I would go on losing more, that the tinnitus was incurable and that I would have to learn to live with it. When I had fully absorbed the significance of all this, I began to sink into an abyss of depression. Would I have to give up teaching? I thought ahead. I was going to lose my hearing, the noise would become unbearable.

I know now that allowing yourself to be demoralised makes tinnitus worse. At the time I had not yet learned this. I began to think that I couldn't hear the television properly, that I couldn't listen to anything on the radio. I lost my appetite, I couldn't sleep properly, often shaking in bed, I seemed to lose interest in everything, I cried for hours.

The new football season opened. I forced myself to Prenton Park. I sat watching Tranmere against Leicester in a zombie-like state, hardly aware of what was going on in front of my eyes.

I dragged myself into school for the 'A' level results. Jane Clark had an A in French and came and flung her arms around me. I hugged her, fighting back tears, a strange mixture of joy for Jane and a general confused despair. Penny Temple looked at me in shock, wondering what on earth was wrong. How I would teach in three weeks' time I had no idea. I went home and tried to prepare some lessons. I simply could not do it.

The phone rang. Dave Leedham, wanting to know the history results. I must have sounded awful. Dave told me to come over, and proceeded to march me nine miles along the banks of the Dee. He tried hard to make me see the more optimistic side: maybe the noise wouldn't get any worse, and the decline in my hearing would be so gradual as not to be noticed. That afternoon, thanks to Dave, I climbed a few steps from the bottom of the chasm.

I found out that the Royal Liverpool University Hospital had an Audiology Department which specialised in tinnitus, and made an appointment with Jacqui Hughes, the Senior Audiologist. Jacqui confirmed by a test that I had lost some hearing, but convinced me that I would be able to go on teaching and that while the noise would not go away, I would be able to cope with it. Further, she promised me that she would ring me after my first day back at school to make sure everything had gone well.

My doctor prescribed dothiepin tablets to combat the depression. Friends Richard and Valerie and my Aunt Ada gave valuable support. I began seeing my current lady friend once more. The thought of Jacqui's phone call was very much a help in my getting down to lesson preparation for the new year. Appetite and sleep returned to normal.

My first lesson in September was with a very low year eight set. Later I was to discover a few behavioural problems in it, but for the present I was simply grateful to feel myself functioning properly again. Confidence returned; I was fluent, I was energetic. Jacqui rang at five. I thanked her for everything. The nightmare was over.

My father had for long been looking forward to the reunion with his Burma Star comrades on the 50th anniversary of VJ day in August 1995. Sadly, it was not to be. Having suffered a massive heart attack and failing to regain consciousness, he died in May. He had always remained modest about his achievements in the war, but I have found out since his death that the missions in Burma on which he found himself as a Chindit were extremely dangerous. There is no doubt that he fully earned his medals.

I remember him fondly for the time he gave me when I was a child, for the love of sport and good music (the light classics, the quality popular singers) he inculcated in me, for the standards of decency he set.

There was one small incident that I have never forgotten which endears me still to him. I must have been about eleven at the time. We were at a fairground in Crewe, on the roll-a-penny stall. The penny I rolled landed clear of the lines in a one-shilling area, but the stallholder claimed the coin was on the line. Dad gently guided me away, with me insisting to him that the penny had been a winner. His reply was:

"I know it was, son, but these people don't have much money. Let's not argue." And Dad himself was earning a very modest wage at this time.

When my mother was dying of cancer in 1962, her sister, my Aunt Ada, nursed her lovingly and heroically through her dreadful final months, spending long hours at her bedside, ready to tend to her needs.

As a boy I spent many a happy morning at Aunty Ada's house, where I was invariably made welcome. She was a very down-to-earth woman, not averse, unlike my mother, to somewhat vulgar terminology now and then. When you arrived at her Casson Street home on a chilly day, for example, she would often greet you cheerfully with:

"Come and warm your arse by the fire!"

Or, if Uncle Albert annoyed her, which frequently seemed to be the case, "Sod off!" or "Arsehole!" would be her regular reaction. Albert, though, was not to be outdone; his revoltingly graphic

"Shit in yer 'and and clap it to!" finished many an argument.

After my mother's death, Aunty Ada was a great support to me, always there with useful advice, sympathetic when things went wrong, rejoicing with me in times of success. She was well aware that I had a stressful job, ever encouraging and understanding when teaching, as it was bound to now and then, got me down. She as much as anyone coaxed me through the low points and kept me running. I invariably took lady friends to meet her, and knew that if she had doubts about them, then in all probability they weren't really suited to me. She would very much have liked to see me marry, but eventually came to accept that for all my liking of female company, this was a fence I would never jump.

Her health was not good in her later years, and following Uncle Albert's death in 1987, she needed the services of a home-help. Eventually she became too infirm to continue living in Casson Street, and her elder son Barry arranged for her to live in a nursing home, where she could be looked after properly.

Aunty Ada lived on until 1996, having grown increasingly frail, until an influenza attack proved insurmountable to her in December. Thus my Saturday or Sunday visits to the nursing home, which had been a highlight of the week for both of us, came to a sad end. Her loving kindness to me, which had endured for over half a century, would be very much missed.

## Chapter Sixteen

In 1971, following the trip to Chinon, I received a letter from Mrs Richards, mother of Stephen, who had been on the visit, thanking Neil Rathmell and myself for helping to make her son's holiday a really enjoyable experience. The letter gave us great pleasure.

An ex-colleague went to teach in another secondary school in the area and in the first lesson duly gave out the text books to be used during the year. When the second lesson began, however, one boy did not have the book with him. When the teacher asked why this was, the boy explained that his mother had thrown the text book on the fire with the remark:

"We don't want that rubbish in our 'ouse!"

Parents, then, come basically in two kinds: the supportive and the unsupportive. At the grammar school, parents were rarely anything less than supportive; at Whitby, after comprehensivisation, the majority showed themselves fully interested in their children's progress. In both schools the PTA thrived, raising thousands for the benefit of the children's education.

However, after 1974, there is no doubt that the number of unsupportive parents, whilst remaining a small minority, did increase. A Stuart House colleague showed me a letter from a parent excusing her son's afternoon absence from school as follows:

"Paul was away on Wednesday afternoon because he went to the pictures with his grandad because it's cheaper for his grandad in the afternoon."

Clearly education was not very high on that family's list of priorities. Likewise this one, whose son was in Hanover House:

"James was away for 2 days last week because he was waiting for the video repair man."

Also from Hanover:

"I'm sorry Lisa was away yesterday. She set off for school, but when she got to the bus stop she realised she'd missed it. She started walking to school, but when the next bus passed her she turned round and went home."

"... Stephen set off for school without his coat. It started to rain, so he went back home and stayed there all day."

"Sorry the girls weren't in school. They didn't feel like going so they went Christmas shopping instead."

This, alas, is what teachers are sometimes up against. But you do get the odd self-critical parent, like this lady with a daughter in Hanover House:

"I am sorry Katie was absent on Friday and that her note was late coming in. I apologise for being a lazy, idle toad."

The former Head of York House, Ann Daniels, recounts a story which shows just how far some parents will go to protect their children from the school's justice. Ann received a letter from the mother of a regularly absent boy who had been away the previous afternoon. The woman excused her son's non-appearance "because of stomach ache." Ann, however, ever suspicious of this family, stopped the boy himself on the corridor and asked him why he had been away.

"I was at the dentist's," he explained, clearly not having read his mother's note.

"Oh really? Which dentist was that?"

"I can't remember."

"Can you tell me where the dentist's is?"

"I don't know."

"You'd better get thinking, then come back and see me at 12.25."

The boy did not appear, but when Ann's phone rang at 12.30, it was his father, an Irish gentleman, somewhat angry at the other end of the line.

"Why are you causing all these problems for my lad?"

"Well, actually I'm rather confused. Your son says he went to the dentist's on Wednesday afternoon, and your wife says he had stomach ache."

"He went to the dentist's."

"Is that correct?"

"Are you calling me a liar?"

"Why didn't he have a note?"

"Because my son didn't know he was going to the dentist's."

"Pardon?"

"No, you see, the dentist rang me up in the morning and said "How are Kevin's teeth?" "

"The dentist rang you up? My dentist never rings me up!"

"Then the trouble with you, Mrs Daniels, is that you don't have a dentist that cares for your teeth!"

A few days later the boy confessed that he had neither visited the dentist nor had stomach ache. He had simply taken the afternoon off.

Here are three further unusual parental letters. The first was shown to me by a maths colleague:

"I don't understand why my son has such a low grade. He has had 50 per cent out of 50 per cent for all his tests."(!)

A quite extraordinary absence note from Stuart House:

"I'm sorry Jason has been absent for three days. He's had diarrhoea through a hole in his shoe."

— and another, from Tudor:

"Tracey was not in school because she has had diarrhoea. It's been all over the road."

Parents' evenings, however, both in the grammar and comprehensive systems, have usually been very pleasant sessions. The majority of the pupils, it transpired, really didn't mind coming to school at all and most parents were grateful for the efforts put in by the staff on their children's behalf. These occasions can, however, be very hard work coming after a day's teaching; you can be asked to talk and listen for up to four hours virtually non-stop, which can leave you fairly close to exhaustion. I once almost crashed the car going home from a parents' evening, entirely through fatigue.

The odd unpleasant person does come along, none the less. A couple came and sat down in front of me at a sixth form parents' evening, and announced their daughter's name.

"She's doing well with her written work, but she's a little quiet in discussions," I said.

"Then you've a problem on your hands, haven't you?" the woman remarked testily, "What are you going to do about it?"

The girl's father, meanwhile, had sat there smiling benignly. I was tempted to say:

"Nice girl, Carol. Must take after her dad!" — but that would have been unprofessional. Carol, by the way, went on to achieve an A in the 'A' level. She simply needed an increase in confidence in her oral work, which she eventually managed to gain. But a domineering mother can't have helped!

A colleague once had a highly embarrassing experience at a parents' evening back in the grammar school days. A couple sat down in front of him, giving the name Lesley Ferris.

"Oh, he's doing well. He answers well in class, his homework's been good ...."

" It's a girl," interrupted the mother.

Keith Muscott had mounted a *Treasure Island* exhibition in his classroom for an Open Evening, when parents were invited to look around the school and view examples of the pupils' efforts. In Keith's case, the children, inspired by Stevenson's novel, had made maps, written essays and drawn pictures illustrating the events of the book. In the background Keith had a cassette telling the story playing discreetly. The display proved popular; parents and children were moving around quietly,

examining the items on show. Suddenly the whole atmosphere was wrecked. A woman whose son had frequently been in trouble and most recently had been nobbled for truancy, causing Keith to write to her, breezed in merrily, declaiming:
"Hello, Mr Muscott! I see our Gareth's in the shit again!"

## Chapter Seventeen

If my teaching during the second half of my career had a little more of the human touch about it than during the first, as I believe it did, then much of the credit for this must go to M... and B... .

Before M my love life had been rather sporadic, hurtling skywards at times, but most entanglements not lasting all that long, especially when the prospect of marriage, for which I had always doubted my suitability, began to loom on the horizon.

M was a widow I met at the house of friends. She was four years my junior, quite tall, reminiscent of country singer Emmylou Harris in appearance, rather quiet, very intelligent, of warm personality, and, when we met, in the process of embracing Buddhism.

She warned me on our first date that she was not seeking marriage; from the start, however, there was an electricity between us which we both knew would sooner or later lead to the sharing of something very special. The Christian principles which had prevented me from enjoying full intimacy with the girls of my early relationships had long since lapsed and M and I seemed decreed by fate to become lovers. A few weeks into the relationship, the inevitable, the irresistible happened.

Then M let me know in the car one night that what she had said about marriage no longer applied. The months went by and our love blossomed, the lovemaking became quite spectacular, ever more expressive and adventurous. I could feel the new confidence I had and the happiness I was experiencing spreading like wildfire into my teaching, and it was from this time that the driving style that I had always cultivated became tempered with a little extra caring for the children in my charge.

One part of me kept telling me to go ahead and propose, but another, from deep inside, held me back, as it were urging me that on no account should I give up my freedom completely. As time went on M began occasionally to show her impatience with my apparent lack of desire for a permanent commitment. The physical side of our relationship, however, remained wondrous, and the rather ungallant thought occurred to me that if I could have love with all the trimmings and still keep a decent percentage of my freedom, then I would be very content with that.

After some four years, however, the relationship began to pall. We began to pick faults in each other, and even the intimacy started to lose its edge. It was M who in the end suggested we call it a day. Perhaps it was just as well, then, that we did not marry. Or would marriage have prevented the decline in our love? Who can say?

If anyone had told me at the beginning of my relationship with B that during it I would a) be chased down a street by a man with an axe or b) be threatened with murder by a second man, then I don't suppose I would have asked her out in the first place.

B was my aunt's favourite carer at the nursing home, tending conscientiously and lovingly to her every need. She had seen me come and go at the weekend and expressed an interest in me to my aunt, who arranged a formal meeting between us. B's smile was most welcoming, her bosom excitingly full, and I began taking her out. Like M she was a widow, like M she had a lot of warmth about her, but the similarities more or less ended there. B was a practical, boisterous woman, totally down-to-earth. And whereas M had been a devout Buddhist, faithfully following the Eightfold Noble Path, B, on seeing some shaven-headed Buddhists manning a table at a Green Fair, dismissed them as "Bloody crackpots!"

Within a short time our affair was ablaze, and I was spending every weekend at B's. Being away from Ellesmere Port at the weekends, relaxing in the heart of the South Cheshire countryside, certainly helped keep the trivial school problems, which sometimes bothered me, firmly in their place. It had been springtime when our relationship began, and the warmer months that followed brought with them an idyll of sunshine and laughter and lots and lots of loving. My post-M blues seemed well behind me now; our summer of sunburnt mirth took me heavenwards once more.

B had paid for her daughter's wedding just before we met, and her wages at the nursing home were very modest. To boost her ailing finances, therefore, I hit on the idea of selling blank video tapes, a large number of which we acquired at a reduced rate in Manchester. A pedlar's licence, therefore, became a necessity, and we went along to Nantwich police station.

"I want to find out about pedlars' licences."

"Why, have you been having trouble with pedlars?"

"No, I want to be one."

I could hear B laughing behind me, but carried on undaunted, and a few minutes later, and £12 lighter, I emerged from the station the proud possessor of the licence. Eventually we managed to sell all the videos and make a nice profit for B. Not without a rather alarming experience on the way, however.

One day we were plying our trade in Coole Pilate, a small village near Nantwich. I knocked on a door, and a rather wild-looking man, his thick grey hair all over the place, opened it.

"Would you like to buy some video tapes?" I asked him innocently. The sound that burst forth from his lips was something akin to an animal's roar; his eyes seemed aflame with fury and he dashed from his door to a trailer parked on the front drive. From this, to our considerable consternation, he took hold of an axe and headed menacingly our way. We bolted back towards the car with our crazy friend, axe aloft, in hot pursuit and leaped aboard, driving off like the clappers with the madman visible through the rear-view mirror, angrily brandishing his weapon in the middle of the road. The danger past, we could laugh ourselves stupid over the incident; at the time it was not pleasant.

The relationship prospered as the months went by. I felt at home at B's and we were having wonderful times together. Once again the prospect of marriage loomed; I knew that B would accept if I proposed. I was due to take B to Paris one summer holiday, and a colleague at school suggested I propose on top of the Eiffel Tower. Once up there, however, I just couldn't do it. The ideal moment passed; now I knew I would never do it. Again the notion of losing my freedom completely seemed foreign to me.

Then an old flame of B's appeared on the scene. He had, B told me, been observing us for some time, parking his car in the lay-by across the road from her house and just sitting there watching for hour after hour. Eventually he rang B up, asking her if I had proposed to her. When she said no, he proposed to her himself! He called her repeatedly during the week when I was in Ellesmere Port, putting enormous pressure on her. For a while it seemed that B would take him seriously, even though their relationship had apparently ended bitterly. I had the strong feeling that B would want to remarry, and I was showing no real signs of asking her. Finally, however, she made it clear to him that she would not marry him, that she wanted to carry on her relationship with me.

He did not take this well, having by now built up his hopes, and told B that he was going to kill me. It was she who gave me the message; I had never actually got to meet my potential murderer. Then B's son, with whom I had always got on very well, threatened to beat up my rival if he showed signs of doing anything to me. Meanwhile I primed the school, giving Ken Oliver in the Junior School and the secretaries in the Senior a full description of my would-be killer's car, and instructing them to ring the police if it appeared on the school premises. Sometimes I had to pinch myself; was this really happening to me, a peaceable, vegetarian schoolteacher?? The car, however, did not appear, either at school or my house. At length my rival seemed to accept 'defeat', and the situation grew less fraught.

But in time B became disillusioned with my seeming unwillingness to discuss marriage, and our amour, having reached the heights, now began to lose ground rapidly. Times together became increasingly unhappy, love seemed to be draining completely away. In the end our parting, sadly, was a relief.

Despite the unfortunate ending of both relationships, however, I will always feel great gratitude to these two ladies; they gave themselves totally to me, taking me to new realms of excitement and fulfilment, and all they asked was that I give myself in return. And whereas for a time I was able to make them incredibly happy, none the less in the final count I had let them down. Perhaps by now, a few years having passed, their bitterness has faded and they are, like me, able to recall with affection the wonderful moments we shared. I hope so, but my conscience remains much less than clear.

# Chapter Eighteen

The return to school in the autumn of 1996 seemed even more stressful than usual. Apart from the task of getting to know new pupils, making sure that lessons were fully prepared and wondering if any of the classes would contain any problem children, there was October to worry about — the arrival of the Rottweilers, as someone termed them, otherwise known as OFSTED inspectors.

As the year began to unfold and I became acquainted with my new classes, it seemed to me I would need a little luck to make a good impression. I had one class on my timetable which had several "dodgy" characters in it; perhaps they would be on their best behaviour when the inspector came in, but really I hoped that I would be visited when I had any of my other classes, which seemed pleasant and cooperative.

The tension mounted as October approached; we all knew we could expect at least two hours of inspectors in our lessons. Heads of Department felt under even more pressure, since their mountains of documentation were due for inspection also.

The languages inspector saw me first with 7T, a form I enjoyed taking, whose conduct was invariably impeccable, but who were sometimes a little slow to ignite. I felt reasonably happy about their performance when the lesson drew to its close.

"You still get a kick out of this, don't you?" was the inspector's first remark. I confirmed that this was true; I knew that it always would be, for as long as I would get a fairly lively response from classes. He was very pleasant, it seemed to me, telling me that he had only just retired from teaching. I had the strong impression that he was very sympathetic to the demands of the job, having only recently stopped doing it himself.

I was half-way through a discussion with the lower sixth based on the idea of "Pourquoi est-ce que la France t' intéresse?" when he walked in again. Once more I felt fairly satisfied, with the possible fault that I had talked too much myself.

When he came along for the third, and what turned out to be the final time, I was about to start a literature lesson with the upper sixth. We were studying a section of *La Gloire de Mon Père*, by Marcel Pagnol. To Simon, Kathryn, Lynne, Emma and Sarah goes my great gratitude; clearly they were straining every sinew to make sure the lesson was successful.

At the end of the week I sensed that overall the department felt fairly happy — a few minor things had gone wrong for some of us, but there had been no total disasters.

A few weeks later the full report appeared. The school as a whole was dealt with first.

> The Whitby County High School is a successful comprehensive school with many strengths and few weaknesses. It is an orderly community in which pupils respond well to the good quality of education provided and to the high expectations of parents and staff.

The report went on to praise the "cordial and constructive" relationships between pupils and staff, among other pleasing comments. Then paragraph 110 ran as follows:

> The teaching of modern foreign languages is consistently good, often very good and occasionally excellent. Teachers are well qualified and have a good command of the languages they teach. They plan their work well, make good use of resources, and have high expectations of pupils. Lessons are varied, lively and stimulating, and conducted in pleasant surroundings in a good atmosphere.

We all felt tremendously boosted by the report. Although by now in my career I was teaching in a confident manner, none the less I was invariably plagued by doubts — Is there a better way of doing this? Am I being too strict? Am I not being strict enough? Have I made sure that everybody has participated? Did I spend too long on that? Was that boy on the back row losing interest? Was the homework I set too short for that class? The list goes on and on. But the report helped us all, I am sure, to feel reassured — even if we well knew that a report on what was after all only a one week inspection could not of course ease all our doubts. At least we now knew that for most of the time at any rate we were on the right lines and our teaching was reasonably sound. And what had seemed potentially a fearsome ordeal turned out to be quite a pleasant, helpful experience.

# Chapter Nineteen

### How Not To

SCENE: Classroom, somewhere near Liverpool. The class, a bottom set year nine, are milling around noisily. Two boys are pushing each other into tables, several of the girls are adorning themselves with mascara and lipstick, talking TV soaps, pop music and boys. The teacher enters. He is in his forties, balding, below average height. His jacket, of a dull brown, looks a crumpled charity shop special.

His tie, a dowdy dark green, is badly creased. His grey trousers have a large black ink stain just above the knee. He has an unsure, timorous look about him. His voice is a little shaky, bordering in its tone on the namby-pamby.

TEACHER: Silence, s'il vous plaît ... (ignored) Silence!
SHARON: Hiya sir!
WAYNE: All right there, sir!
TEACHER:(feeling desperately unconfident) You're supposed to say it in French, remember!
WAYNE: Oh yeah! Bonjewer monsewer!
TEACHER: Monsieur, Wayne, monsieur.
WAYNE: That's what I said— monsewer!
(hubbub carries on. Teacher desperate, starts to shout, but unconvincingly)
TEACHER: Silence! Silence! S'il vous plaît!
WAYNE: (threatening) Look yous lot! Sir's ready. Siddown, right! Jones, siddown or I'll bleedin' thump yer, right?
(silence gradually descends)
TEACHER: (humbly) Merci, Wayne. Et maintenant, ouvrez vos livres. Page trente, exercice trois.
WAYNE: Right, you do as he says ... Page thirteen.
TEACHER: No, Wayne, page thirty.

WAYNE: Oh yeah! Page thirty.
TEACHER: As you can see, this exercise is what's called a gap-fill ... (noise at back) ... Philip, quiet, please ... (boy still talking) ... please, Philip Smith, quiet!
WAYNE: Button it, Smith!! (Smith goes quiet)
TEACHER: Merci, Wayne ... now, where were we? Ah, yes ... each sentence has a blank in it, and what we have to do is to fill it in. Do you all understand? (general lack of interest. One boy reads a comic under his desk) Lee White, what are you doing?
LEE: I'm listening to you, sir.
TEACHER: And what else?
LEE: Oh, I was just looking up a word in my French dictionary, sir.
TEACHER: Très bien! Now, if we can look at the first sentence, we read "Je blank la télévision." Now, can we all put our thinking caps on and suggest a right answer? ..." Je blank la télévision" ... (no response) ... Come on now, who's going to be the first with a right answer? ... (with enthusiasm) Remember, there could be more than one correct answer!
JEFF: How bloody excitin'!
TEACHER: What's that, Jeff? Répète, s'il te plaît.
JEFF: I was just sayin' how much I like writin', sir.
TEACHER: Admirable, Jeff! We'll be getting our stylos out, shortly.
SHARON: They can't touch yer for it!
TEACHER: Silence, Sharon, s'il te plaît. Jeff, suggest something for our sentence.
JEFF: Football.
TEACHER: Pardon? Je ne comprends pas.
JEFF: Football. Je football la télévision.
TEACHER: But Jeff, football is not a verb!
JEFF: Not a what?
TEACHER: A verb!
JEFF: What the 'ell is he talkin' about? All I know is there's football on telly. That makes my sentence right!
OTHERS:(noisily) Yeah, Jeff's right!
Be fair, sir!
Jeff's gotta be right!
TEACHER: Silence! Silence! Silence! 'Football' is not an action word!
JIMMY: Of course it is, sir, I 'eard 'em on telly. "Welcome to today's football action."

TEACHER: You're all wrong! (getting very desperate) You're so very wrong!
JEFF: Prove it then!
TEACHER: A verb is something like 'eat', 'drink'... .
KAREN: Je mange la télévision!
TEACHER: No, Karen, no! C'est quoi en français, 'watch' ?
DENISE: Une montre, monsieur.
SHARON: Smartarse!
JIMMY: Swot!
JEFF: Knowall!
TEACHER: No, Denise, a verb, a verb! Let me demonstrate a verb! The verb 'throw', for example. Look, if I were to throw something ... (gesturing)
SHARON: (excited now) I'll do it, sir! A paper aeroplane! (tears paper from exercise book)
TEACHER: Wait, Sharon, no! (Sharon makes aeroplane, projects it across room)
OTHERS: Great one, Sharon!
Yeah! Yeah!
Can we all make one, sir? (more paper torn off, more missiles thrown)
TEACHER: Please wait! Stop! Please! Please! Help me, Wayne, please!
WAYNE: Right, yous lot, stop! Sir's had enough of that. If anyone else throws one, I'll ram it down yer bleedin' throat, all right?
(gradually calm descends, but the floor is now strewn with paper planes. The Headmaster walks in.)
HEADMASTER: Ah, Mr Simpson ... good grief, what's been going on in here? Why is your classroom in such a state?
TEACHER: (weakly) We were demonstrating verbs, Headmaster.
HEADMASTER: Oh really? See me in my study at break, would you? (exits)
TEACHER: (almost crying now) Now, year nine, look what you've done! Now I'm in trouble with the Headmaster! Oh dear! Now I'm really beginning to get angry! And when I'm really angry, the sparks will fly!
SHARON: (mocking) Don't scare me like that, sir!
KAREN: (pretending to chew finger nails in fright) You're terrifyin' me, sir!
LISA: (mock swooning) You're my hero, sir. You're so dominant!
LEE: Christ! Another hour wasted!

PHILIP: What a wanker!
WAYNE: Sorry, sir, but even I think you're pathetic!
(Teacher sinks into chair at the front, totally defeated. Bell goes; class storm out.)

## Chapter Twenty

The school's musical activities have gained enormous distinction over the years; they have also given me, as a regular listener, great pleasure and a feeling of pride in the school.

Malcolm Perry was Head of Music from the school's inception in 1959 until his early retirement in 1982. Malcolm was a noted composer himself and was interviewed on Radio 3 about his cantata, the mighty and ambitious *Turn Back, O Man*. Malcolm scored this for tenor and baritone soloists, chorus and orchestra, and it was performed for the first time by the Ellesmere Port Music Society (which Malcolm has conducted for some forty years now) in the school hall in March 1967. The work is a comment on twentieth century man's materialism, using the parable of the prodigal son as its text, along with poems, one of which was written by EPGS sixth former John Thomas. The local press reporter called the cantata "a religious experience ... moving and compelling."

I particularly recall the Christmas concerts that Malcolm organised, the outstanding choral work, the subtle lighting in the hall and his very imaginative and effective use of the school foyer (just off the hall) where the choir was positioned to sing such items as *The Infant King* and *The Coventry Carol*. And how the hairs on the back of one's neck responded!

Malcolm's other noted compositions included a tuneful suite *Fiesta*, a choral piece *Ring Out Wild Bells* and *Canzona* for brass.

Under Malcolm's dedicated tutelage many excellent young musicians developed their talents and went on to successful musical careers.

· John Gough is without the slightest doubt the most gifted pianist in the school's history to date. At a very young age he composed the incidental music for the school play *An Italian Straw Hat*, and his performances in concerts were startlingly good when he was only twelve years of age. John is now a tutor at the Royal Northern College of Music and a regular performer on radio, television and the concert circuit. He can also be heard on CD and cassette. John's cassette *En Route to Lotus Land* has deservedly proved a heavy seller; it is a charming collection of miniatures mainly from the twentieth century, with the pianist revealing a prodigious technique and a delightful delicacy of touch.

John Gough recently appeared in the role of Jacqueline du Pré's accompanist in the feature film *Hilary and Jackie*, and composed the theme for the TV drama *A Sense of Guilt*.

John is lavish in his praise of Malcolm Perry:

"Inspirational. Gave so much, so freely, yet remained so unassuming. Always calm — there were never any explosions."

And as Malcolm helped bring John's talents to full fruition, so John, in his turn, passes on his own gifts generously to his students, several of whom have reached the television finals of 'BBC Young Musician of the Year'.

Ed Smith was a born entertainer, a fine player of euphonium and French horn, whose love of music, nurtured by Malcolm, would last a lifetime. He became Chief Executive of the Birmingham Symphony Orchestra when it was conducted by Sir Simon Rattle.

Cornet player Alan McDonald went on to star on Swedish radio, and oboist Philip Thomas, after doing theatre design work with John Piper, no less, became Head of Education at Opera North, outreach musician for the Royal Liverpool Philharmonic and historical and architectural consultant to Bridgewater Hall in Manchester.

Melanie Orriss was an outstanding flautist, going on to reach the semi-finals of the Young Musician of the Year competition. Robert Davis proved a promising composer at school, notably of atmospheric piano pieces, but achieved greater fame as a writer (using his school nickname Rib Davis) of plays for Radio 4. Excellent contralto Jane Lennie is now a regular solo concert performer.

On occasion the school choir would join forces with that of our German twin-town Reutlingen, and in the seventies Haydn's *The Creation* and Handel's *The Messiah* were performed in Chester Cathedral. In the Philharmonic Hall in Liverpool the school choir had the privilege of being conducted in concert by Sir Charles Groves and Sir Simon Rattle.

Stephen Watson, who has served the Maths Department honourably for many years, has proved himself also a classical composer of considerable talent. A CD of his music, containing his impressive cantata *O Captain, My Captain*, his tone poem *Autumn Boughs* and his *Symphonic Study* (my personal favourite— a lovely piece in the traditional English pastoral style) has sold several thousand copies. *Autumn Boughs* has been performed by the Hallé Orchestra in the Bridgewater Hall.

Michael Williams and Anne Rushforth were the leading figures of the eighties and nineties.

Mike, who retired from working at the school in 1998, became Head of Music in 1983. His tastes were extremely catholic, and a school concert under his aegis was just as likely to include something by Neal Hefti or Duke Ellington or by Jerome Kern or Paul McCartney as it was pieces by Mozart or Debussy. Mike's passion for all kinds of music never seemed to falter; the devotion and zeal he brought to everything he did at Whitby, his tirelessness, the unstinting encouragement he gave to his protégés, made his contribution to the school's life enormous. He was first-rate as a teacher (gaining a top grade from OFSTED in 1996) and a composer.

Mike's compositional output is large and varied. He had his anthem *Glory and Honour* performed in Wells Cathedral, and his *Missa Brevis* was premiered in Liverpool's Anglican Cathedral in August 1998, conducted by Malcolm Perry. He also composed an orchestral suite for Shakespeare's *The Taming of the Shrew* and an orchestral fantasy based on *Gaudete* as well as numerous settings of poems for the Girls' Senior Choir. Mike has further set verses of W. H. Auden for piano and contralto, and Jane Lennie premiered this work at Burton in 1998.

In conjunction with lyricist Leigh Stanley (an old boy of the school) Mike has written melodic musicals *The Glass Slipper*, *A Christmas Carol*, *Charlie and the Chocolate Factory* (with Roald Dahl's enthusiastic approval) and *Flotsam and Jetsam*.

Ex-pupil James Hodkinson spoke thus of Mike:

"He had a great knowledge of musical history and theory and a very broad cultural background. He was so creative, such a good arranger. He gave his all in making all different forms of music accessible to his pupils. Always so modest— he will probably hate reading this!"

I used to put Mike on the spot regularly in the staff room, whistling a few notes from a symphony or a concerto and challenging him to identify it. These proved so easy to him that I soon realised I would have to dig up something pretty obscure to have a chance of defeating him. One day I was sure I would have his measure; I had been listening to a rarely heard symphony the evening before, and whistled him four notes from its final movement.

"Could it be Honneger's third, fourth movement?" asked Mike after about two seconds. Amazing!

A further Ellesmere Port-Reutlingen scholastic joint venture saw the performance of *A German Requiem* by Brahms in Chester Cathedral, and recent years have brought inspired co-productions between the Music and Drama Departments such as *Bugsy Malone, Annie, Cabaret, Grease* (the puritan in me still objects to some of the lyrics in this) and *Oliver!*. Estelle Buckley, Gareth Anderson and Joel Parry have revealed notable musical and dramatic talent in these.

What a pity for the school it is that not only Mike but also Anne Rushforth have now left it. Under Anne's guidance the Senior Girls' Choir reached incredibly high standards of musicianship, performing with enormous credit at the Llangollen Eisteddfod and the Newtown and Warwick festivals, and being voted Merseyside Choir of the Year in the *Liverpool Echo* Competition.

Samara Bryan, a member of the choir at the height of its achievement, could not praise Anne enough:

"She was inspiring, she made you feel a winner. She was strict but friendly, and the choir had a family feel about it. She taught us to perform not just with our voices, but with our eyes and our expressions as well. Being in that choir was terrific!"

Jennie Murphy, a very promising young singer who was encouraged to audition (successfully) for the Cheshire Youth Choir after singing with distinction with Anne, is equally enthusiastic:

"She was great. She made you work hard, but it was enjoyable— it didn't seem like work. I was proud to be a part of our choir!"

Every girl immaculately turned out in white blouse adorned with red rose and long black skirt, every face smiling, every bright and eager eye trained irresistibly on its adored leader, the joy, the enthusiasm of their singing, the gorgeous rich sound that they made, the Whitby Senior Girls' Choir under Anne Rushforth coruscated in the artistic life of the school like a diamond.

At the advent of the comprehensive school, Bob Fox became Head of Drama. The Junior Hall quickly became a well-equipped drama studio (although it must be underlined that this was a converted assembly hall rather than a purpose-built drama studio which some schools enjoyed at this time) and it was soon apparent that a new era was born. The annual school play continued, though these became rather more spectacular than previously, but what Bob Fox wanted to achieve was not just the production of a showpiece that would involve the élite; his aim was to open things up, as it were, to present something that was representative of the drama work done in the school, something that would involve larger numbers than formerly. As well as the annual play, therefore, Bob Fox brought in the annual drama festival, a large-scale production to be done in the round, as a celebration of drama rather than a competitive event between houses. This featured literally hundreds of performers, every one of whom seemed trained to perfection with never the slightest chance of anything going wrong. I have a clear image of the finale of one of these events, in which over two hundred children gathered on the set carrying lighted candles, to quite astounding effect. The level of self-discipline that was inculcated into the participants was incredible! Because of the vastness of these productions and the huge numbers involved, Bob acquired the nickname 'Twentieth Century Fox' in some quarters of the staff room, which no doubt amused him.

Bob Fox's flair, drive, perfectionism, technical skill and imagination led to outstanding productions in the school; *Elidor, Hiawatha, The Hobbit, The Royal Hunt of the Sun, The Golden Masque of Agamemnon* and *Song for a Dark Queen* brought the school great prestige. Mark White, David Barker, Gareth Pritchard, Paul Farrington, Graham Trevor, Rachel Nightingale and James Hodkinson were among those who blossomed as actors under Bob Fox's direction, turning in performances of maturity.

After Bob's departure, John 'Big Daddy' Welshman (tonsured very much like the late wrestler) was appointed Head of Drama. He was a fine actor, as I had seen for myself several times at Heswall Hall, and an excellent director, well-liked and highly-rated by his students. Unfortunately John's career at Whitby was plagued by ill-health, but one of its undoubted highlights was *Much Ado About Nothing*, in which Joel Parry, Samara Bryan, Anthony Watson and Richie Nimmo distinguished themselves.

Di Sanna took over the department after John retired and a startlingly powerful *The Crucible*, featuring a gripping performance by John Gardner, was the last play I saw as a teacher in the school.

Another charismatic young actor to impress in this Arthur Miller play was Matthew Yeoman, who was also, under Mike Williams' guidance, showing enormous promise in music as a composer, pianist, arranger and singer. I am confident we shall hear much about him in the future; it seems on the cards that Matthew will become another distinguished old boy of the school.

Between Ron Durdey and Di Sanna 35 years had passed; I had seen a large number of productions of infinite variety, which had brought the school a fine reputation and given acting and backstage opportunities to several hundred pupils. I value the enormous efforts put in by staff and pupils in the staging of these plays which, like the sport and the music, gave me the fascinating opportunity of observing away from the classroom young people I knew and appreciating their talent in a different domain.

## Chapter Twenty-One

Every day at Whitby was hectic, which had the advantage of making the day's labour seem to pass quite quickly, and yet, on the other hand, usually left you feeling very weary when you actually stopped work. In my final year, at the age of 56 and 57, due to the general tightening up process, I taught more hours and had less free periods than in any other year in my whole career. I tried to do all my marking for years 7–11 in school, which often necessitated staying until 5.30 or 5.45. Sixth form work I did at home, which meant that on some nights I had to mark or prepare after evening meal; a twelve hour working day, therefore, was not a rarity. During the periods of internal exams, that day could be even longer.

Here are the full contents of a typical day.

*November 10, 1997*

Arrive at school 8.5, collect daily bulletin and mail from staff room tray.

8.10 Go to classroom. Prepare materials needed for the day. Get out cassette recorder needed for lessons one and five. Get out overhead projector and have transparencies ready for lessons one, three and four.

Get model house ready for lesson two. Have flashcards of house ready for lesson two and town places flashcards ready for beginners' early lesson and lesson three. Have list of Paris attractions ready for lesson five. Have toy transport items ready for lessons one and four. Have cassettes and discs on hand for music shop sketch, lessons one and four.

8.30 Beginners start to arrive for early lesson. My invariable early morning nervousness, which no amount of experience would ever change, begins to dissipate after I greet the first few in.

8.40 Register beginners. Read the bulletin to them.

With OHT, teach class the French names of places in Ellesmere Port town centre. I name the places, they repeat; then round and round we go until they can name all fifteen.

9.0 Dismiss beginners. Year 8 (lower set) arrive.

Using models (like most of my realien, cheap buys at car-boot sales), teach methods of transport. Class slow to awaken; I keep driving away, eventually response better. Then transparency of musical instruments: teach the vocab, then extend into phrase, eg Je joue du clavier (I play keyboard). Then we work on a scene in a shop where they have pretend to buy a disc or a cassette. Fair result, but will need more practice next lesson. Then aural exercise — they have to listen to a cassette of a cycle race and follow the course on a map in their text book. I collect homework.

10.5 Dismiss year 8. 7Y arrive, a class I have just once in the week. One or two of the boys need watching, but mostly a likeable class who respond quite well. Using model of house (also from car-boot sale), teach rooms, then reinforce with flashcards. Then they describe their own houses.

11.10 Dismiss 7Y. Break, which seems to go so quickly that I never bother trying to spend any of it in the staff room; drink a cup of water.

11.20 7T arrive. I like this class.

11.25 Lesson three begins. Teach them the higher numbers, 70-100. Reinforce with mathematics in French. Then OHT of Ellesmere Port, teach features. Hammer away until well known. Collect homework.

12.25 Dismiss 7T. Down to staff room for lunch — sandwiches.

12.50 Return to classroom, start marking.

1.10 Register a class for absent colleague. Since I teach the beginners' course on some mornings, I do not have my own form.

1.20 Return to my room. Year 8 (top set) arrive. Good class for oral work— a few weak at writing.

1.25 Lesson 4 begins. Revise transport with models — pleasing. Switch to transparency on directions (right, left, straight on, etc.). After several minutes' practice, give 'live' aural test on these, checking they can understand the way to places in town. Then they prepare a scene: a combination of an interview on their musical tastes and the purchasing of a CD or a cassette in a shop. Ten minutes given to prepare, while I tour the room listening to each group, then they perform in front of the rest. It goes quite well.

2.25 Dismiss year 8. Welcome year 10 — a top set; not bad, pleasant, though a few of the lads frisky on Monday afternoons. Give out list of Paris attractions. Discuss, with a view to preparing imminent Paris project. Then play cassette for aural work on French workplaces. Revise perfect tense. Give back previous test and review it. Collect homework.

3.30 Dismiss class. Start marking.

5.35 Finish marking. Tidy room. Put equipment away. Go home.

# Chapter Twenty-Two

When Jacqui Hughes left the Audiology Department at the Royal Liverpool University Hospital to move to a new position at Alder Hey, Mary Daly became my audiologist. I went regularly for consultations and hearing tests, which I always dreaded in case Mary could see serious problems just around the corner. For a few years, however, Mary, dissipating my fears, would say something like "I think you can carry on a while yet", and I went away happy.

At the end of 1996, though, she warned me that although she thought I could do one more year's teaching after the current one, the summer of 1998 could be the time to stop. I began to accept this gradually, knowing that if I could get that far (I always feared a sudden deterioration in my hearing, but Mary assured me that was not likely), I would be 57 and many of my friends had retired from teaching before that age. It would also mean that I would have fought for over five and a half years with tinnitus and impairment, which would represent some sort of victory over the handicap.

Some children, especially timid first year girls, speak so quietly that even a young teacher with sharp hearing would have problems with them; this thought had always to be borne in mind. But as time went on I knew that my situation was proving more difficult to handle. Consonants were the problem; I was becoming unable, for example, to tell whether a child had said 'six' or 'dix'. Further, conversations with the French assistants were getting harder for me: I was missing a fair amount of what they were saying. Watching French films was similarly affected. I was also becoming dishonest, pretending to have heard what a pupil had said when in fact I had not understood part or all of it. There was one class I had which had three quietly-spoken girls on the back row; I realised at the end of one lesson that although I had asked everyone else in the room a question, I had not asked them any, fearing that I might not have understood the reply.

I explained all this to Mary in early 1998. She gave me a test and confirmed a decline since my previous one, which, although 'slight', was enough to signify that attempting year 1998-9 would not be advisable. Mary told me she would write me a full report which I could use in my application for early retirement, which was duly submitted in March. By May the county had granted my leaving.

By now all my friends and most of my colleagues knew of my problem, and were sympathetic. I find that most people these days have heard of tinnitus and know what it is. Some, though, have failed to master the word.

"How's your tetanus?" I have been asked more than once.

"How's your titinus?" is another amusing variation.

For me the worst time of the day is the first few minutes after waking. Then the noise seems so loud that it can be quite alarming, causing me to wonder how on earth I am going to hear anything at all that day. The best thing is not to linger in bed, but to get up and exercise. By my last year in teaching I had a routine of yoga, aerobic and anaerobic exercises worked out which lasted an hour and a quarter, and which helped not only with the tinnitus but also to combat the general stresses of a day's teaching. The tinnitus usually starts to settle as the first active hour of the day begins to unfold. I have to say that the tinnitus has never, so far, prevented me from falling asleep (although the depression brought on by it in 1993 had done), but now and then I have woken up in the middle of the night thinking that it was absolutely pouring down outside only to find on pulling back the curtains that the pavements were bone dry. The sound of heavy rain had been all in my head.

Naturally I have often wondered what caused my affliction. From all that I have been told or read, the primary reason for it is probably listening to music played too loud on a headset. How unfortunate it was that by the time I was aware of the danger the damage had been done. It must have been around 1980 when I started using the headset; therefore I had been pounding my ears quite mercilessly for some twelve years when they let me know (by the distorted Rachmaninov) that they could take no more. Now, needless to say, the headset has long been discarded and when I listen the volume remains at a modest level. I can still get some pleasure from recorded music; stringed instruments do not normally distort in my ears, thus string quartets, classical guitar pieces and bluegrass music are still pleasing to me at a moderate volume. Orchestral classical music is a problem with its wide range of sound; if I raise the volume when I can't hear a pianissimo section, then the level becomes uncomfortable during fortissimo passages. These days discos (regular haunts with both M and B — on reflection, they can't have done me much good) are taboo, likewise big-band concerts, but I can still enjoy live small group jazz, most chamber music and some country music, as long as the room in which it is being played is not too small.

If there was one thing that I had learned from 1993 it was that although my handicap was unfortunate and a bloody nuisance, the depression that I suffered from in that year was far worse; one thing I determined on now was that I would not sink into it again. Instead I threw myself wholeheartedly into my final few months of teaching, which, despite my problem and its occasional embarrassment, I probably enjoyed as much as any part of my career. I suppose this is partly a psychological phenomenon, since you know that if you only have to continue doing something for a short while, then you can hurl yourself at it with abandon. I tried to make a joke of it when my hearing let me down, breezing through the problem, and the pupils, it must be said, did not try to take advantage of the situation.

My year eleven class contained many students I had known for four years, others for two years, and I was fond of all of them. I particularly wanted them to do well in the new format GCSE, and some five weeks after I had left I came into school to see how they had fared. I felt the same old terror as I walked in — thirty-odd years had failed to change this —

but a few minutes later joy and relief, undiminished by the passage of the years, flooded over me; they had done well, several surpassing their estimated grade.

At the end of June a rather boisterous party was thrown in my honour at Penny and Bill Temple's house, with lots of singing and excellent fare. Their home is notably spacious, with a sizeable conservatory and a large garden containing a huge pond; it makes an ideal venue for parties, and Penny and Bill are generous, hospitable hosts. There had been several departmental get-togethers there over the years.

Jealousies and bitterness within departments are sometimes evident in schools, but there were in fact very few contretemps in the Languages Department. I think we were all aware that the job was difficult enough to do without adding to its stresses by squabbling.

Carol Howard had by now been its Head for three years, cheerfully and effectively coping with the vast amount of work that came her way, invariably well-organised, and doing a great deal to knit together its French and German components, whilst carrying skilfully a considerable teaching load. I could never have taken on what Carol did — she had my fullest admiration. The modern day Head of Modern Languages in a typical large comprehensive school has indeed a fearsome burden to bear.

After Steve's departure in 1994, Nikki Perry had become Head of the French branch of the department. Over my 35 years I saw literally hundreds of teachers come and go, but I can say without doubt that Nikki was in some ways the most remarkable I ever saw. She was quite small in stature, but somehow she had the ability to gain perfect control over classes containing known trouble-makers who were a handful for other teachers. And she rarely had to resort to outbursts of temper or bawling and shouting to do it. She had the Svengali stare; one steely look was usually enough to dissuade anyone thinking of doing something she didn't approve of. I had seen many firm disciplinarians in action in the school over the years, but none had quite the awesome presence of Nikki.

She was extremely orderly, too, always able, for example, to put her hand on any important piece of paper she had been given, even if this had been months previously. She cared, too; for other staff (she would help anyone with a problem, no matter what department they belonged to) and for the pupils, who, although they were in awe of her, knew none the less that in case of difficulty or a personal problem, she was there for them.

Mike Cleaver was a very gifted member of the department who worked his socks off for the good of his pupils. He was known to shout now and then if someone crossed him, but the vast majority of his students recognised that they were getting quality teaching and being given every chance of obtaining a result at the end of it. Mike seemed able to conjure top grades out of the most unlikely characters, so well did he prepare them.

Shauna Holloway was always modest about her abilities, but totally unjustly so. I watched her teach a full lesson three times and her quiet style was every bit as effective as that of the more flamboyant language teachers. Her rapport with the pupils was excellent and her caring approach helped to make her a notably fine teacher of lower sets. Shauna's ratings from the OFSTED inspector were astronomical! And no matter how hard-pressed she was, Shauna always had a smile that would lighten anyone's day.

Debbie Tacon, as generous-hearted a person as you could ever wish to meet, was a versatile teacher, expert in both French and German, and very gifted as a PSE tutor. Debbie came out well from the inspectoral visit, and was another who cared a lot for her flock. I know that her year eleven French class of 1997–8 thought the world of her.

Helen Chamberlain had just completed her second year when I left. No matter how long one has been in teaching, one can always learn from others, including, I have often found, new or newer members of staff. Helen to me seemed surrounded with an aura of serenity. Still susceptible to occasional outbursts myself, it was quite humbling for me to think that someone of so little experience could remain so calm. Helen, totally dedicated, had already proved herself an excellent young professional.

1997-8 was to Kevin O'Rourke what 1963–4 was to me, except that Kevin came out of his first year's teaching rather better, I suspect, than I did. He was already thoroughly involved in the German exchange with Reutlingen, and it is very heartening to see young teachers like Kevin showing the amount of commitment they do, always prepared to come in very early and stay very late to try to make sure the job is well done.

Sponsored Day came and went, then Sports Day, with a pleasing invitation to come back and do the commentaries in 1999. Cards and presents started to come in, people said very nice things to me, and the end approached.

On July 17th, 1998 I set out to teach for the last time at Whitby High School.

## Chapter Twenty-Three

I had seen teachers reduced to tears on their last day at school; these included the supposedly iron-hard Billy Hannah at Crewe Grammar. An image of him sitting there sobbing after his final assembly remains ever clear in my mind. I tried to resolve that no matter what happened I would keep my emotions in check and would therefore have a final day I would be able to look back on without embarrassment in the years to come.

I had been asked by the P.E. Department to present the prizes at the year eight sports assembly, but it was only towards the end of the assembly that it was whispered across to me to say a few words when the presentations had been completed. I improvised a while about making the most of one's sporting abilities, mentioning our alumnus Rob Jones as an outstanding example.

First lesson was year ten, a word game I had devised with a prize for the winner. I felt surrounded by their warmth towards me, and I will treasure their cards as a souvenir of a class with lots of personality and friendliness.

7W followed, how to buy an ice cream in France, possessive adjectives and finishing with a numbers game. This class will always have a fond place in my memory. From the outset in September they caught fire, providing me with hours and hours of entertaining satisfaction, and every one of them was as likeable as you could wish. It was always marvellous to have a class you could do virtually anything with, with no fear that anyone would turn stupid; 7W were such a class.

They had also been involved (along with 7Y) in charity work during the year, helping to raise a good amount of money for the Blacon Animal Sanctuary, near Chester, and taking four of them to Blacon to deliver the cheque and piles of food for the animals a few days previously, when they had had the pleasure of meeting a lot of the cats and dogs, had been a joy; watching them fussing over and playing with the animals, being licked and jumped on repeatedly to their great delight, made the effort well worthwhile.

I had only three lessons that day. I was free in the afternoon and a notice board check told me I hadn't been taken for a substitution. 7T were to be my final lesson.

They began coming in when the end of break bell sounded at 11.20. Usually they went straight to their seats, but now they gathered around my table. A box of chocolates, a bottle of wine and a card that all of them had signed appeared in front of me. I felt twenty-odd pairs of eyes upon me, expectant and, dare I think it, affectionate. I hope that my own warm feelings for them showed through as I thanked them for their kindness. They went to their seats, the lesson began. Word games, numbers games, prizes and laughs. Then "Au revoir, la classe" for the last of what I calculated must have been in all about twenty-five thousand times.

A Stuart House staff party ensued over the lunch hour, given by Keith and his current deputy Laura Feather. Keith and I had worked together amicably for fourteen years as Head and Deputy of Stuart, and we recalled happily now the days of the show, the carol singing and the characters, both staff and pupils, who had passed through the house. Being a Head of House in a large school can be very wearing; you never know what your work-load is going to be on any given day. Parents ringing up, teachers sending undisciplined children to you, extra administration jobs coming your way — Keith coped manfully with it all, never losing his sense of humour or of proportion.

In the afternoon I said goodbye to Mr Fletcher, to colleagues, to the school nurse Hanse Colenso, who had helped me with good advice on tinnitus (and proved an excellent masseuse of cricket injuries), to the dinner ladies, to the caretakers Brian and Bill (both, mercifully, much more cheerful than Bubble), to my favourite cleaner Aggie, who had done my room for many years and who had now forgiven me for the masks incident, and to the eternally hard-pressed but unfailingly obliging office staff. A chat with Russ and Ken, then home to pack for the French trip, which would leave at midnight. My farewell speech had had to be recorded; I gave the cassette to Ken, who would play it at the staff meeting the following week, when I would be in Brittany.

I arrived home just after half past three. I had survived. I hadn't broken down or become undignified. There were more cards behind the door which had arrived in the post. It was a strange feeling, a confused mixture of joy for the kindness that had been shown me and unutterable sadness that my time at the school was over.

There were the occasions when I could have cursed the pain-in-the-backside pupils who can mar the atmosphere in the classroom or who will simply not try hard, contributing nothing to the lesson, who seem less interested in their career than the teacher is! Yet far more often I found myself feeling grateful to every pupil who ever put his or her hand up in my lesson, who ever got 10 out of 10 in a test of mine, who ever greeted me with a cheerful smile, who ever took the trouble to produce a good homework, who ever made me laugh with a funny remark, who ever made me think that I was contributing, doing something worthwhile. And if a lesson has gone well, there is no feeling quite like the thrill of having ignited a class, having communicated and educated and perhaps had fun at the same time. There had been so many, many times when I felt so fulfilled, so happy, as if I had quaffed deeply of the rich wine that life can sometimes offer, that the bad times, the times of total exhaustion and frustration, the times of wondering whether to go on, now seemed comparatively insignificant.

I am content now that I chose to be a teacher, and if I had my time over again I would make the same choice. I would change my first few months, plus a small number of uneasy moments along the way, but for the most part I would be happy to live it all again.

I had kept my emotions under control all day, but now, as I was about to remove my jacket, all it took was the touch of my finger on a piece of chalk in my pocket for an explosion of grief to hit me. I cursed the problem that had cut short my career; all I wanted at that moment was to be able to go back to school in September, to teach again, to feel still part of the school, my school, and not to lose the cordiality I had felt displayed to me in it.

This thought was destructive and had to be curtailed; I couldn't go back now, and I had to accept the situation. After all, I had had 35 years in the school; I had numberless fond memories, many good friends from it who would still be around, and the satisfaction of having made a modest contribution to its life. And having to be back at school at midnight for the trip to Brittany certainly helped to refocus my thoughts.

# Chapter Twenty-Four

Somehow a kind of enchantment fell over the 1998 trip to Brittany; exploring the pretty town of Plancoet, our base in the north-east of the province, after dinner on the first evening of our stay, with its trim park, quaint streets and gentle river, set the trend. The next morning, as the sea glistened in the sunlight and we headed west along the scenic coast towards the small port of Paimpol, the spell seemed to continue. From Paimpol, the ferry to the Ile de Bréhat, with its rocky coastline, its car-free little lanes, its easy-going air, and the hustle-bustle of school seemed aeons away.

It was already becoming clear to us, too, that the pupils we had with us were going to prove one of the best groups we could remember. The coach driver passed comments on the good manners of the youngsters he had spoken with, the hotel staff likewise. It is never possible for a teacher to relax totally on a school trip. There is always the chance that someone may get separated from his or her group of friends and become lost (this happened once on a snowy day in Paris, but mercifully had a happy ending); that someone may get hurt on the road or become ill— there are various possibilities. I have always found that ironically the only time you can let go and enjoy it fully is in retrospect, when it is all over and everyone is safe home again. But in so far as a teacher can appreciate a trip while it is actually happening, I think that all four of us (Mike, Nikki, Debbie and myself) enjoyed this one as much as any.

As the week progressed the happy memory bank for the future grew fuller; the afternoons on the beach at St Cast and St Lunaire, with Jamie dropping all the shrieking girls into the sea; Fougères castle, where the handsome young guide captivated several of the girls and the historic little town of Vitré where a sudden storm soaked most of us to the skin; Dinan with its ancient steep streets, St Malo's ramparts and attractive shops; the evening's bowling at St Brieuc; the fun around the hotel pool, the competitions and the prizes, the meals together ... six days to remember with affection.

On the journey back from Cherbourg I went on deck for some time; several of our party came to chat for a while, then I was alone. On every trip I'd been on there had been the feeling that the return journey marked the end of being what was, essentially, part of a family for a few days, which, for a bachelor like myself, gave a novel taste of what 'real life' (that is, the family situation with responsibility for children 24 hours a day) was like. It was a taste I usually liked; whether that was because it contrasted interestingly with my normal way of life or whether I really was a family man manqué I am not sure. That feeling came upon me again now; our "beautiful children," as Anne would have called them, would soon be back with their families once more and the spell would be broken — this time for ever; the end not only of this trip, but the end of everything. Thirty-five years would draw to a close in a few hours' time. I felt a deep sorrow invading me, taking me over, at one and the same time a quite exquisite yet almost unendurable emotion. In a sense it was a kind of dying I was going through, an agony of losing something good, something I had to let go, no matter how much the letting go hurt... .

I finally returned to the lounge, where some of our party were gathered. One of our girls was sitting just behind the teachers' seats; Beverley, a year nine pupil. I had not known her at all before the trip, but during the previous six days she had made a very favourable impression. She had an alert, intelligent look about her that would brighten any classroom, making me wish I could have had the good fortune to have taught her myself. Part of my duties in Plancoet had been to conduct a French speaking test with each pupil and Beverley, despite having done only one year's French compared to the three years of her friends, had acquitted herself very well. She had also shown enough self-confidence to take part in a quiz game in front of fifty spectators and had sufficient skill and sang-froid to become one of the winners.

I had further noted that she could take care of herself when any male members of the party annoyed her or paid her more attention than she wanted. On the beach or in the hotel grounds she was the healthy youngster playing or chasing around with her friends; in the evening, at the dining table, wearing her nicest clothes, she metamorphosed into a radiant, very feminine young lady, immaculately groomed and possessing an engaging smile. She had also, it seemed to me, already a good degree of poise, with a natural, unforced manner, and she was totally unfazed by the fact that her group had to share a table with the teachers.

I turned to her now, and a conversation began to develop. She seemed quite happy to tell me all about herself and I, welcoming some relief from the painful gloom that had enveloped me, was more than content to listen.

She spoke of her family, leaving the strong impression that she was very close to them; mum and dad, her elder sister Karen (16) and a younger one, Diane, aged seven; then of her animals, causing me to wonder where the humans lived in this house containing two dogs, a cat, a budgie, a gerbil, some rabbits, some fish and even a snake!

Beverley told me she was born under the sign of Taurus, and confessed to being stubborn; after almost a week with her I now knew for myself that she had other supposedly Taurean traits—she was reliable, sociable and went about everything with an abundance of joie de vivre. She seemed to like school and was obviously doing well, although she remained modest about it; I knew from Debbie that she was very good at German, her first foreign language. Later in the summer she would be going to Minorca with her family, so that, never having been abroad before France, she found herself going twice within a few weeks, which pleased her a good deal.

Finally I asked her if she had any ideas about her future career. She had, in fact, not just ideas, she knew for sure. Beverley was going to be a teacher. She told me that from as far back as she could remember teaching had been the only career she had ever dreamed of pursuing. As a young child she loved to play 'school' and she always acted out the role of 'teacher'. She used to write out simple sums and spellings on her mini-chalkboard and pretend that her dolls and teddy bears were her pupils!

When Beverley was seven, her mother gave birth to a third daughter, Diane. Diane was born three months prematurely (weighing just 1lb 13oz at birth and having to be wrapped in tinfoil to ensure survival) and needed constant stimulation, both physically and mentally, if she was to have a chance of developing at the same rate as other children of her age. Beverley spent a lot of time with her, helping her, passing on her knowledge to her and gaining enormous satisfaction from doing so.

Beverley's mother later told me much more about this. Diane suffered from croup as a baby, necessitating a tracheostomy, an operation in which a hole is made into the trachea through the neck to relieve the obstruction to breathing and a plastic or rubber tube inserted. Diane needed the tube for the first four years of her life, and Beverley and Karen learned how to change it for her. Linda Henning could not praise enough the love and

*Beverley*

devotion Karen and Beverley brought to the task of helping to bring up their little sister. Linda told me that she herself tended to be rather overprotective of Diane (understandably), and it was as if Karen and Beverley sensed this, knowing that Diane could do more physically than her mother was allowing her to do. At first to Linda's alarm, but later to her eternal gratitude, Karen and Beverley had Diane doing handstands, cartwheels and forward rolls like any normal child would, instinctively aware that there was no real risk involved.

"They were brilliant with her, absolutely brilliant," says Linda now.

They also helped Diane to learn to write and with her early progress in mathematics.

This feeling of having been a positive influence in someone else's life reinforced the early desire Beverley had had to teach, and now, seven years after the arrival of her baby sister, she was fully (and remarkably maturely) aware of the possibility of influencing young children in her care for the good, of sowing seeds from which, hopefully, they would reap benefits for the rest of their lives. I was moved by what Beverley had told me; clearly she wanted to be a teacher for the purest possible motives and nothing, it seemed, was going to stop her.

In her quite delightful company, my sombre mood had somehow dissipated, my obsession with my own sense of loss had abated. My interest in Beverley, especially in her very firm plans for her future, had brought an unexpected uplift.

My own career was over, the time had come for me to leave the stage; similarly, all over the country there would be countless teachers departing at the end of their careers, teachers who had given the best years of their lives for the benefit of young people. And who would replace them? Serious shortages, it seemed, were imminent; the outlook was not good. Yet here was one of those very same young people, waiting in the wings, already fully committed to her future, prepared to do the same herself, to take on the load, to battle through the frustrations, to devote herself to the cause, willingly, enthusiastically, lovingly. Here was a girl who filled me with hope and not a little admiration.

Three cheers for Beverley Henning.

# Epilogue: And So To Bev

Thursday 20 May, 1999. Rossmore Primary School, Ellesmere Port. Beverley is on the fourth day of her work experience as a classroom assistant. An art lesson. She helps two children with their paintings of ships, then moves around, assisting individuals with various drawings. She looks at home here, patient, affectionate, conscientious, as if this was what she had been born to do. And the children clearly like her. The bell goes. Most of the children have finished the work and hand it in before going out to play. But a few haven't. Beverley goes around to these less fast workers, giving them all the attention they need, helping them through, happy to be there until the last one has completed the task.

Class teacher Sarah Tinsley confirms Beverley's very promising start.

Later Irene Proudlove, the Whitby teacher sent out to observe and report on Beverley, speaks very favourably: "Totally committed, very relaxed and comfortable in the environment. The pupils produced very good work with her. The school was very impressed."

Bev's dream is on its way towards coming true.